American Commonwealths.

TEXAS

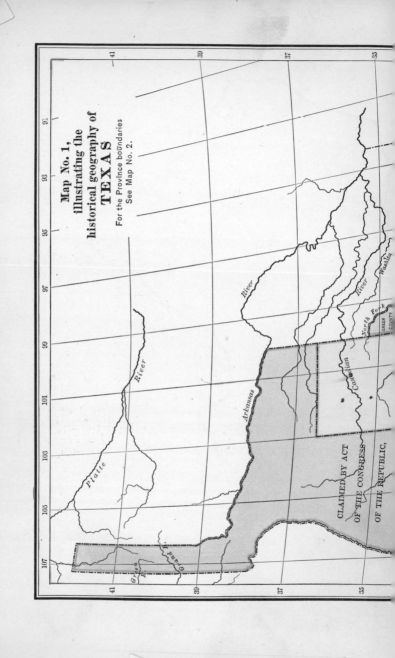

Map No. 1,
illustrating the
historical geography of
TEXAS
For the Province boundaries
See Map No. 2.

Platte River

River

Arkansas River

Green River

Grand River

North Fork

Canadian River

Washita River

GREER COUNTY

CLAIMED BY ACT
OF THE CONGRESS
OF THE REPUBLIC,

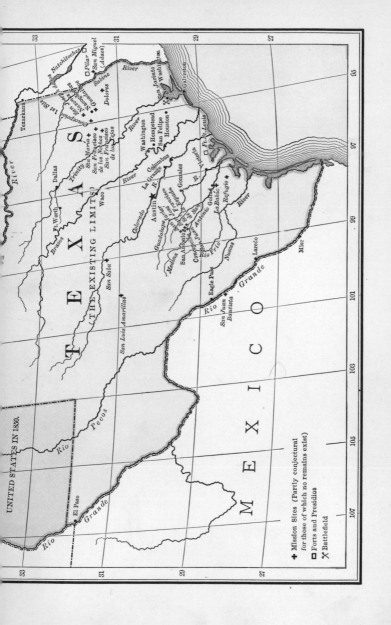

TEXAS

A CONTEST OF CIVILIZATIONS

BY

GEORGE P. GARRISON

204

Published May, 1903

PREFACE

THE reader will please remember that this book is not intended for a history of Texas. It is rather, to use the words of the lamented Dr. Scudder, the original editor of the Series, "A study based on [that] history." My aim has been to give a picture of what Texas is, and of the process by which it has become such. With this in view I have, for the most part, neglected details, and have dwelt mainly upon the salient features of the experience of the people under consideration. My special object has been to reveal the significance and the effect of this experience.

My judgment has been that the purposes of the work would be best served by avoiding a systematic citation of authorities by means of footnotes. It has, however, been written under a keen sense of responsibility for every statement and every reasonable implication. However short of absolute accuracy it may have fallen, that has nevertheless been the standard aimed at in the writing. But there is

yet a vast store of unworked material for Texas
history, and many periods in the life of the Province, the Republic, and the State are still obscure.
Through some of these it is necessary, until now,
for those even who know most of the subject to feel
their way. The authorities and sources used are
to be found in the various collections accessible in
Austin, and the fairly trained investigator wishing
a check on the correctness of the narrative can
easily locate the passages on which any part of it
may rest. If errors have crept into the book, —
and there are doubtless enough of them, — I shall
be glad to have them pointed out; but I trust it
will not become necessary to change extensively,
in essential points, the presentation here attempted.

Some difficulty has been experienced in dealing
with the question of accenting Spanish proper
names that have become familiar in English. The
usual custom of English writers hitherto has been
to omit the accents. Spanish scholars, however,
have adopted a simple and convenient system of
accentuation, which it seems to me should be extended, as far as practicable, to the words adopted
from that language. The Spanish *tilde* cannot
safely be omitted, any more than the French quali-
tative marks which are regularly written, and the
accent is quite as important. Neglect of it has

already fixed certain popular errors in pronunciation in Texas, *e. g.* An'a-huac for A-na'huac. I have followed the usage of the Spanish Academy as far as possible without making it obtrusive. I have not tried to correct Anahuac, nor have I ventured to give the proper Spanish brand to the sacred name Alamo, but I have always written Espíritu, etc.

The book is not large, but this has not saved the writer from having to ask the help of many in the various aspects of its making. I am under special obligations to Professor W. J. Battle, Miss Lilia M. Casis, Dr. Herbert E. Bolton, Mr. Eugene C. Barker, and Mr. E. C. H. Bantel, all of the University of Texas; Peter J. Hamilton, Esq., of Mobile; Professor John R. Ficklen of Tulane University; Judge C. W. Raines of Austin; Mr. R. C. Clark of the University of Wisconsin; Mr. E. W. Winkler of Brenham; Miss Elizabeth West of Bryan; and Judge Bethel Coopwood of Laredo. My acknowledgments are due also to Professors F. W. Simonds and T. W. Page of the University of Texas, and Mr. R. A. Thompson, engineer of the Texas Railroad Commission.

GEORGE P. GARRISON.

UNIVERSITY OF TEXAS,
April 15, 1903.

CONTENTS

TEXAS

CHAPTER I

EUROPEAN EXPANSION IN AMERICA

To understand aright the making of Texas, one must see it in its proper historical relations as a part of the process by which the peoples of Europe occupied America, and which has culminated in the formation of the American Union and its dominance on the Western Continent. It is easy to see that, from the standpoint of general history, the Revolution of 1776 is but the transition to a new stage of this process. Monroe's famous annual message in 1823 officially asserted that the period of colonization from overseas was at an end; but this did not stop the flow of population, nor the shifting of political boundaries with the advance of the United States. Now the great American Republic, not content with having expanded from the Atlantic to the Pacific, has added to its dominions Hawaii, Porto Rico, and the Philippines. What the future will bring it, none can tell, nor is it necessary here to surmise. For the purposes of this book it will be sufficient, first, to see the outlines of this movement in its entirety in order to grasp its meaning; and, second, to observe how from it has arisen Texas.

In the discovery and exploration of the New World the Spanish led the way. After the daring first voyage of Columbus had established the scientific theory that the East might be reached by sailing westward and had dissipated the terrors with which superstition had covered the face of the Atlantic, he and his successors soon found their way to the mainland of South America. Gradually they extended their voyages entirely around the Caribbean and the Gulf, along the opposite Pacific coast, and up the Atlantic as far as Virginia; and De Soto and Coronado led far into the unexplored wilds of the Mississippi basin expeditions that have been a lasting puzzle to investigators, but which in substantial results were fruitless.

While yet the Spanish had hardly more than begun their work, the English came and sailed along a portion of the Atlantic coast. They were first to reach the mainland, but they soon retired from the field and left it to the French. These found their way up the St. Lawrence, and ultimately around among the Great Lakes and down the Mississippi to its mouth.

Meanwhile in the track of the explorer had come the colonist. Early in the sixteenth century Spanish settlements had begun to dot the shores first seen by Columbus and his companions, and within less than thirty years from the discovery Mexico had been conquered. Spain had now acquired a good base for colonization on the mainland; but the work, considering its importance, was carried on with little energy. The larger part of South America, where there was practically no competition except from Portugal, was won with comparative ease. To the north, however, there was more to fear. In that direction the outposts were thrown far forward. Mission, presidio, and vill were scattered northward, as time passed, through the valleys of the Rio Grande, the Gila, and the Colorado, along the Pacific coast, and thinly here and there over the whole Southwest. But the land was not really occupied, and the few weak and widely dispersed settlements acquired strength much too slowly for the needs of the after time.

Early in the seventeenth century the French took up the work, and planted colonies along the St. Lawrence and the Lakes and in the country adjacent. Finding the north coast of the Gulf of Mexico, to which they were led in following the Mississippi, still unoccupied, they established settlements, of which the oldest permanent one dates from 1699, in the vicinity of the great river's mouth, and set up a claim to the vast region which it drained, and which they called Louisiana. But, like the Spanish, they spread themselves over more territory than it was possible for them to hold with such a light sprinkling of population, and their path-breaking enterprise was turned finally to the advantage of their hereditary enemies, the English.

Almost exactly at the time when the French were making their earliest settlements in the Northeast and the St. Lawrence valley, the English estab-

lished on the Atlantic coast two groups of colonies,
a southern and a northern. They did not, like the
Spanish and the French, range far and wide in
search of gold or trade, nor concern themselves in
any high degree about the souls of those Indians
whom they did not kill. On the other hand, again
unlike the Spanish and the French, they began at
once to wring a living from the soil and the neighboring sea, and ere long a little surplus to exchange
for whatever the vexatious navigation acts of the
English Parliament allowed them to obtain hon-
estly, or the enterprising smuggler brought them in
defiance of such acts. At the outset, they seemed
content with relatively narrow limits; but, to avoid
any dangerous concession to their rivals, they extended their claims westward to the Pacific, though
they knew little of the distance, or the geography
of the unexplored region beyond the mountains.

Into the unoccupied section between the northern
and the southern group of English settlements, or,
roughly indicated, the country bordered by the
Delaware River and Bay and the Hudson, pushed
the Dutch and Swedes, starting a group of colonies
that became in after times the four Middle States.
The Dutch took possession of the Hudson and made
the original settlements in what became New York,
and on the Delaware they were first to settle within
the limits of the later New Jersey. The Swedes
established colonies that constituted the beginnings
of Delaware and Pennsylvania.

As the work of colonizing went on, there grew

out of it that series of struggles for possession the most remarkable feature of which has been English and Anglo-American expansion. In 1565 came the preliminary conflict of the series. It was between the Spanish and the Huguenot French who were seeking a refuge in Florida. It was bloody and brief, and it ended in breaking the hold of the French on that part of North America forever. This affair, however, was essentially rather an episode of the counter-Reformation in Europe than a contest for territory. It was nearly a century later before the energy which was spending itself in the religious wars in Europe began to be diverted towards America and to show its effects there. During the latter part of this interval the English, Dutch, and Swedes had established themselves along the Atlantic coast in the fashion already described, and it was in that quarter that the next group of the series of struggles occurred. In 1655 the Dutch began the movement with an easy conquest of the Swedish colony on the Delaware. In 1664 a similar conquest gave to the English the country in possession of the Dutch, including the settlements on the Hudson and the Delaware, both Dutch and Swedish. In 1673 New York was retaken by the Dutch, but in 1674 it passed finally back to the English, who thus filled the gap between their northern and southern colonies and made of their territory a single continuous strip lying between the Alleghanies and the sea.

But the real struggle was between the English

and the French. It came with the great series of
European wars following the accession of William
and Mary in England, and ending in the overthrow
of French supremacy in Europe, and the transfer, from France to England, of an empire more
substantial in its potency than any the world had
ever seen. At the conclusion of the contest in 1763,
the English possessions had expanded westward to
the Mississippi, southward to the Gulf of Mexico,
and northward as far as the land was worth claiming; the French were practically excluded from the
North American continent; and the Spanish, whose
interests had led them to join the losing side, had
been deprived permanently of the territory they
claimed in Georgia, and temporarily of Florida, but
had obtained by way of compensation Louisiana
west of the Mississippi, and a fragment, including
New Orleans, to the east of it.

In 1776 the English colonies joined in declaring
themselves independent of Great Britain, and by the
treaty of Paris in 1783 their independence was fully
established. They were no longer simply a mouth
by means of which England might devour America;
they were a separate political organism, which had
inherited all the appetite for territory of its parent.
Although their population had yet hardly begun to
flow across the Alleghanies, through bold diplomacy
they succeeded in winning by this treaty the country westward to the Mississippi, so lately torn from
France. Soon their experience taught them that
in order to enjoy the full benefit of this acquisition

they must control the navigation of the river that gave access to it from the Gulf; and seizing the opportunity when the remainder of the valley, which Spain was unable to hold, was taken back from her by Napoleon, who then needed it less than the money it would bring, they were enabled to buy it in 1803 at a price hardly worth naming.

Meanwhile the French and Spanish had clashed, in rather feeble and irresolute fashion, in the border land between Louisiana and Mexico. A French colony planted by mischance on Matagorda Bay in 1685, and a commercial expedition sent by the governor of Louisiana to the Rio Grande in 1714 had roused the Spaniards from their neglect of the country north of that river. The founding of a few scattered missions was sufficient to secure them possession. The French were more easily displaced in that quarter than they had been in Florida. The country thus weakly colonized by the Spanish was formed into a province in 1727, and acquired more or less definite boundaries with the name of Texas. But although the Spaniard had taken possession of the land he feared the French might win, his title was still in dispute, nor was it fully recognized till 1819. By the treaty between the United States and Spain made in that year, the claim which the French had based on the settlement made by La Salle in 1685, and which had passed with the Louisiana purchase in 1803, was given up as part of a general bargain by which Florida was acquired, and the way for the Anglo-American to the Gulf on the south was completely cleared.

In 1821 a revolution, begun in 1810, whose original occasion had sprung from the French occupation of Spain during the Peninsular war, and whose final impulse was received from the rising of Riego and Quiroga in 1820, culminated in the separation of Mexico from Spain. During this period, and even earlier, Texas had been an inviting field for those who love the excitement of revolutionary agitation, and various filibustering expeditions, composed mainly of Anglo-Americans, were directed thither. But after Mexico became independent, its government inaugurated a more liberal policy towards immigration, and the Anglo-Americans came peaceably in large numbers, brought in by *empresarios* as colonists. In a few years they became the dominant element in Texas. They could not adjust themselves to Mexican methods of government; in 1835, unable to endure it any longer, they rose in revolt, and in 1836 they finally threw off the Mexican dominion. The new-born republic at once sought annexation to the United States; but for nearly ten years, because of opposition from the anti-slavery element in that country, it had to stand alone. Texas, however, was too great a prize, and too willing to be won, to remain independent. The expansion impulse at length prevailed, and annexation, the Mexican war, and the acquisition of the whole Southwest followed in rapid succession. The Teutonic civilization had made another notable encroachment on the Latin, and Texas had been enabled to bring a history peculiarly its own, short in time, it is true, but rich in achievement, to merge in the greater record of the American Union.

The observant reader will see at once that this conspectus serves as a general explanation of the making of Texas, not simply in a geographical, but also in a social and political sense. The spread of revolutionary ideas in Mexico and the separation from Spain gave a new impulse and a different direction to the national life, but the Spanish element in Mexican civilization was not essentially reduced. The coming of the Anglo-Americans and the overthrow of Mexican sovereignty brought about a much more radical change, but did not entirely wipe out the Spanish influence even in Texas. This influence has, in fact, left ineffaceable marks, not on the Texan character, perhaps, but certainly on the institutions of Texas, especially on its system of jurisprudence. All the peculiar social forces that have helped to determine the life of the Province, the Republic, and the State must be included in accounting for the result as it exists. The Texas of to-day can be understood only through a knowledge of its development, the origin and external relations of which have been briefly presented in this chapter. It now remains to consider a little more closely the process itself.

CHAPTER II

PRE-COLONIAL EXPLORATIONS OF THE TEXAS
COUNTRY

THE land which now goes by the name of Texas
is a district of irregular shape, 265,780 square
miles in superficial area. It reaches from 26° to
36° 30′ north, and from 93° 30′ to 106° 30′ west.
Its southeastern boundary is the shore of the Gulf
of Mexico. In a geographical and topographical
sense it consists of a number of belts or benches
nearly parallel to the Gulf coast, each somewhat
narrower in the middle than at the ends. The whole
series rises gently northwestward to the great plateau of the Llano Estacado, the northern part of
which reaches an elevation of over four thousand
feet. The larger rivers of the district all have a
general southeasterly direction. None of them is
important for navigation. The flora and fauna
are of a transitional type, between the characteristic forms of the Appalachian and the Cordilleran
systems. There are immense forests of large timber in eastern Texas, while in the central part are
extensive prairies, and farther southwest and west
is a comparatively barren strip lying along the Rio
Grande and widening as it extends up the river.
This strip is low and flat next the Gulf, but be-

tween the Rio Grande and the Pecos it becomes broken and mountainous, some of its peaks being over nine thousand feet in height. A considerable part of the upper end of it is within the limits of New Mexico, while eastward of the upper Pecos it contains the plateau of the Llano Estacado already mentioned, of which the eastern half lies in Texas. Reaching northward between Oklahoma and New Mexico is the rectangular projection of Texas known as the Panhandle. The primary and evident adaptabilities of the section are for agriculture and stock raising; but of its natural resources in detail there is more to be said later.[1]

It was nearly two hundred years after the discovery of America before this country had a name, or, in fact, boundaries definite enough to claim one. It might have been otherwise but for the fact that these were such busy centuries in Europe. Within less than two years after the first voyage of Columbus, France and Spain, which were just passing from feudal disorganization into the unity of national statehood, began to match their new-born strength in a contest for possession of the weak and divided principalities of Italy. This contest was closely followed by a succession of confused and general European wars, due to the rivalry between the French kings and the Hapsburgs; and these, through the working of the Reformation, were gradually converted into a series of religious struggles that ended only with the practical disso-

[1] In chapter xxiv.

lution of the Empire at the peace of Westphalia
in 1648. In the same year that Cortés began the
conquest of Mexico his youthful king became the
emperor of Germany. Thenceforth Charles was
too much engrossed in preserving and strengthening his imperial inheritance from the Cæsars to
realize the splendid possibilities of America. His
successor as king of Spain, Philip II., was not
gifted with the ability to recognize great opportunities, and even if he could have understood that
which he had in the New World he could never
have improved it while he exhausted his resources
in fighting the battles of Catholicism. During his
reign the defeat of the Armada broke the power
of Spain, its decline began, and its chance to win
America became thereafter less and less; but it
still clung to the policy of wasting its strength in
European wars and neglecting its interests in the
West. Meanwhile England, wrestling with the
devil and with itself, making martyrs alternately
of Protestants and of Catholics, and fevered with
the raging antipathy of Puritan and Cavalier, was
passing through one of the most intense periods
of its history. After the peace of Westphalia
Europe had scarcely a breathing spell before the
nations lying around France found it necessary to
combine against the ambitious schemes of Louis
XIV. One of these schemes it was, in fact, which
roused a weak energy of expansion in New Spain
and led finally to the birth of Texas in the latter
years of the eighteenth century.

During this interval, however, the Spanish explorers, though working slowly, had not been altogether idle. Little by little the veil was lifted from the Southwest, and bit by bit the true geography of the Caribbean and Gulf and the adjacent lands was brought to light in the maps embodying the results of successive expeditions by sea and land. In his first voyage Columbus sailed for some distance along the northern coast of Cuba. In the third (1497) he reached the mainland of South America at the point where the line of the Lesser Antilles, the eastern limit of the Caribbean, diverges from the coast. Two years later Ojeda followed the southern shore of this sea from there to Cape Vela, near the western boundary of the present Venezuela, and in the winter of 1500–1501 Bastidas and Cosa traced it thence to the Gulf of Darien. In his fourth voyage (1502) Columbus reached the coast of Honduras and passed along the shore of the Caribbean from there southeast to the Isthmus. In 1513 Ponce de León landed in Florida and gave it a name, and ran the entire length of the outer side of the peninsula and the inner as far up as Tampa Bay, and later in the same year Balboa crossed the Isthmus and discovered the Pacific. In 1517 Francisco Hernandez de Córdoba led from Cuba to Yucatan a slave-hunting expedition, which sailed west and southwest along the coast of the Gulf to a point a little way beyond Campeche. The reports carried back to Cuba by the survivors of this expedition led Governor Velasquez to fit out another, which he placed in charge of his nephew, Juan de Grijalva, and which was dispatched in 1518. Grijalva extended the exploration of the coast to the mouth of the river Pánuco. In 1519 the remainder of the Gulf shore, that is, the part lying between the Pánuco and the upper end of the Florida peninsula, was explored by Pineda, acting under the orders of Garay, governor of Jamaica.

In the same year, 1519, Cortés began the conquest of Mexico, and the city was finally taken in 1521. By 1523 the whole country south, from Pánuco on the Gulf coast and Colima near the Pacific to the Isthmus of Tehuantepec, was under the control of the Spanish.

The success of Cortés aroused the envy and jealousy of many influential Spanish leaders, who wished to have the continuation of his enterprise committed to themselves. While their efforts at widening the area of the Spanish dominion were not brilliant with results, they succeeded in paralyzing his own; and thus the work, that, under a competent general and with unity of plan, might have been accomplished in a few years, was spread over three centuries, and was never thoroughly done. It began on the Pacific coast and was gradually extended north and northeastward. The tide of conquest and political organization rolled with wearisome slowness towards the Rio Grande. One by one Nueva Vizcaya (from the northern part of which was later formed Chihuahua), New Mexico,

Coahuila, and Nuevo León emerged into more or less definite provincial existence. But as the Spanish arms and civilization came in closer contact with the wild and fierce Apaches and Comanches of the north, their progress became increasingly difficult and uncertain ; and until within the last quarter of the seventeenth century there was no Spanish settlement east or north of the Rio Grande except Santa Fé, and no other, in fact, in the whole of the northern Gulf shore region between that and San Augustine on the eastern coast of Florida.

During the earlier decades of the two hundred years while the New World Scythia beyond the Great River of the North was still left to the savage and the bison and whatever living thing the wilds had nourished, the Spanish imagination had flown thither and returned with tempting legends to invite the Spanish adventurer. The Indians told the conquerors, in language which they could but poorly understand, tales which must have been framed to meet the evident wishes of the hearers, and which were doubtless embellished on repetition to suit the designs of would-be *adelantados*. The atmosphere of New Spain was exceedingly favorable to the production of myths, and they grew rapidly ; the most important being that of the Seven Cities of Cíbola in the unexplored country to the north, which were reported to be exceedingly rich and populous. This tale was much used by the enemies of Cortés to further their designs in opposition to his.

While the story of the Seven Cities was on the tongue of every Spaniard in the land, there arrived in Mexico in the year 1536 three white men and a negro who told one of the most extraordinary tales of shipwreck, suffering, captivity, and ultimate escape that ever fell from mortal lips. The most prominent man of the party, Cabeza de Vaca, afterwards wrote a detailed account of his experiences. The four were survivors of the Narvaez expedition, which had been sent out from Spain to subdue and govern Florida, and the remnant of which had suffered shipwreck on the western shore of the Gulf in the year 1528. After an awful experience of about seven years in slavery among the Indians, they had run away and finally reached the Christian settlements in Mexico. They were apparently the first Europeans to tread the soil of Texas, and they brought the earliest information as to the inhabitants and the character of the yet unchristened land.

To Cabeza de Vaca and his companions the country was a part of Florida, which, by the commission of Narvaez, included the Gulf coast to the river Pánuco ; but the remoteness of the Spanish settlement on the east, and especially the French seizure of the mouth of the Mississippi, naturally joined it, when possession was obtained, with New Spain.

The four involuntary explorers who had come from beyond the Rio Grande had seen no rich and populous cities, but they had heard of some which had many people and very large houses. Though it was but little that they could add to the current story about Cíbola, their coming aroused a new interest in it. The viceroy, Mendoza, sent a friar, Marcos de Niza, to ascertain if he could what truth there was in the tale. Niza went on this errand in the year 1539, leading a party which included the negro Stephen, one of the wanderers with Cabeza de Vaca. Starting from Culiacán on the Gulf of California, they traveled in a general northerly direction, and finally reached Cíbola, which has been identified with one of the Zuñi pueblos in western New Mexico. Stephen, who went in advance, reached the pueblo, but was not allowed to enter, being lodged outside the walls. His misconduct aroused the hostility of the Indians, and they killed him. Niza, therefore, did not venture into Cíbola, but only saw it from the top of a neighboring hill. He went back, however, with extravagant accounts of the size and wealth of the place. It is difficult to believe that his description was not colored to suit the wishes of Mendoza and of Coronado, whose interest in the matter will appear below.

The outcome was what Mendoza had planned, an expedition for the conquest of Cíbola. Cortés desired to lead such an expedition himself, and so did Guzman and De Soto ; but the only effect of their efforts to secure the command was to prevent the appointment of any of them, and to leave the management in the hands of Mendoza, who appointed as its leader Francisco Vasquez de Coronado, governor of Nueva Galicia. In 1540 Coronado led forth from his province a strong and well-equipped force into the northern wilds. With his two years of wanderings and conquests and the disappointment of both himself and Mendoza over the unsubstantial results of the expedition, we have nothing here to do. The one fact to be noted in this connection is that his route must have carried him across the northern part of what is now Texas.

Subsequently the country was penetrated by explorers at various points while it was yet unsettled and nameless. De Soto must have passed through the northeastern part of it in 1542, and in 1582 and 1590 respectively Espejo and Sosa penetrated to the valley of the Pecos from the west. In 1601 and again in 1611 Governor Oñate of New Mexico made expeditions eastward which must have carried him into Texas; and in a little more than four decades after the latter date there had been made from the same province, according to the records, a half dozen visits or *entradas* directed towards the country of the Jumanas and the Quiviras that could not have failed to lead the padres or soldiers who undertook them through the same section. An *entrada* of 1650, led by Captains Hernan Martin and Diego del Castillo, is said to have penetrated to the Tejas tribe of Indians; and in another in 1684 Padre Nicolás Lopez and Captain Juan Domingo de Mendoza conducted a party of missionaries and soldiers from El Paso down the Rio Grande to the mouth of the Conchos and thence into the interior across the Pecos to a *ranchería* of Jumánas and Hediondas.

Before this time there had been established the oldest town within the present limits of Texas. Simply because it is the oldest, it deserves a passing notice. It began as a village of Tiguex Indians, who were friendly to the Spanish, and who were driven from Isleta in New Mexico by the rising of 1680. They were settled by Governor Otermin in a pueblo which was within twelve miles of El Paso, and which was also called Isleta [1] after the name of the New Mexican settlement the Indians had been forced to abandon. It could have had no Spaniards among its population other than one or two padres, and for this reason it cannot be properly regarded as a Spanish colony. It has had no important share in the life of Texas, which has grown from another quarter; but it has had a continuous existence dating from the year 1682.

[1] In the spelling of this name as applied to the town in Texas, the old form, Ysleta, has prevailed.

CHAPTER III

Fort Saint Louis

THE delay of the Spanish was the opportunity of the French. During the two centuries of slow and feeble advance by their rivals in the Southwest, they found their way along the St. Lawrence to the Great Lakes and down the Mississippi to the door that Spain had left ajar. In 1535 Cartier sailed up the former river till he was stopped by the rapids now known by the name of Lachine. One by one the lakes were discovered, and in 1673 Joliet and Marquette made their way from Green Bay on Lake Michigan, by Fox River and Lake Winnebago, after a short portage, to the Wisconsin, and thence to the Mississippi. They followed this river as far down as the mouth of the Arkansas, and then, for fear of the Spaniards, went back the way they had come. But La Salle, starting with a party of about fifty followers in December, 1681, passed from Lake Michigan by way of the Chicago and the Illinois to the Mississippi, and in the spring of 1682 reached its mouth. Elated by what he called his discovery, and ignorant or regardless of the fact that the Spaniards had anticipated him therein by about a century and a half, he called the country Louisiana and claimed it for France. Then, as early as possible, he made his way to Paris with the purpose of organizing an expedition to return and secure possession of the long neglected land. Louis XIV. was just at that time nearing the high tide of his aggressive policy. He had men and money to employ in extending French power and influence in any part of the world, and it was not difficult for the enthusiastic explorer to obtain a share for use in seizing the Mississippi valley and subduing the Spanish colonies in New Spain.

In the summer of 1684 La Salle started back to America. The king had given him more ships than he had asked, and had put in charge of one of them a captain of the royal navy. This man, by name Beaujeu, though under La Salle's orders, was the better seaman of the two, and did not hesitate to quarrel with his suspicious and irritable chief, and between them they brought the undertaking to disastrous ends. It was the intention of La Salle to establish a fortified post near the mouth of the Mississippi, that would control the navigation of the river and thus give security to French settlements in the upper part of the valley; but he missed his destination, and, after various mishaps, landed early in the year 1685 at what is now Matagorda Bay on the coast of Texas. This, in spite of evidence to the contrary, he took for one of the mouths of the Mississippi; so he established on the shore a temporary camp.

La Salle had started with four ships. One was captured by Spanish buccaneers in the West Indies, one was wrecked in seeking to enter the bay, and soon after the landing Beaujeu sailed for France with the third and most important, thus leaving but one for the service of the colony.

It was soon ascertained that the bay on which the French had landed had no connection with the Mississippi. It therefore became necessary to select a better location for the quarters to be occupied until the original destination could be discovered, and the party conveyed thither. The choice fell on what La Salle considered a satisfactory spot, about six miles from the head of the bay on a river emptying therein.

The river on which the settlement was fixed La Salle called La Vache, and the Spaniards, with unusual tolerance, simply translated the name into Lavaca, and continued to use it. The fort built for the defense of the colonists he called by his favorite name, St. Louis, which he had given to another establishment planted by himself on the Illinois River in 1682, and which he gave also to the neighboring bay. The Spanish, however, gave the bay to which their attention was drawn by this settlement the name of Espíritu Santo, and sometimes they called it alternatively San Bernardo.

As the buildings at St. Louis went up, disease was busy among the colonists, and before the end of the first summer thirty of them had embarked for the final voyage of all mankind. The reader,

sitting secure and afraid neither " for the pestilence
that walketh in darkness, nor for the destruction
that wasteth at noonday," will be, perhaps, little
moved by the recital of this fact; but when the
imagination restores the true original color of the
picture it becomes heart-breaking. With constant
toil and privation the lot of all; with treacherous
and cruel Indian enemies always at hand; with the
outraged Spanish expected day by day; with escape
impossible; and with Death, meanwhile, making his
ceaseless round from couch to couch, what more
could men have been expected to do and suffer?
Yet this was but the prelude to a more heroic history, in which desperate courage and unfailing
endurance, self-devotion untainted by self-seeking,
and self-sacrifice without the hope of reward became
almost too common to invite attention and record.
Moreover, the pitiful truth, which must be told, is
that those who were buried at Fort St. Louis during that fatal summer of 1685 were most of them
victims, not of hardship nor of an insalubrious cli-
mate, but of their own beastly self-indulgence; and
that the colonists, whose sufferings might win them
so much sympathy had they deserved it, were few
of them worthy of respect. Joutel, the historian
of the expedition, and himself a member of the
company, says, " they had all been caught by force
or surprise; " and some of them proved themselves
in the course of time to be most absolute villains.

When the colonists had been sufficiently provided with shelter and protection from enemies,

La Salle set out to find the Mississippi. He left in October, 1685, and returned in March, 1686, but without having accomplished his object. In April, 1686, he started on a second journey, aiming to make his way in search of help by the Mississippi and the Illinois to Canada. He reached the Cenis [1] Indians, a tribe belonging to the group known as the Tejas, on the Trinity River, where he was attacked by a fever that delayed him two months; and when he recovered he found it necessary to return to Fort St. Louis. In January, 1687, he went forth to make another attempt to reach Canada, and had gone nearly as far as in the journey previous when he was assassinated by some malcontents among his men.

The settlement at Fort St. Louis survived about two years longer. When the Spaniards finally reached the spot, in the year 1689, they found the buildings empty, and looking as if they had been plundered but a short time before. Three dead bodies, one of them that of a woman, lay on the adjacent prairie. Four men who had belonged to the colony were found among the Indians in the neighborhood with a small party of roving Tejas, and they reported that the destruction was the work of a band of savages.

Thus came to its end in disastrous failure the first European settlement made on the soil of Texas. It was the outcome of a bold and splendid plan soon afterwards consummated in the French pos-

[1] Called by the Spanish Asinais.

session of Louisiana. Its founder was one of the foremost of those brave spirits who, working, as is the common lot of heroes, not for themselves but for all mankind, tracked the far-reaching and perilous wilds of interior North America and won a continent for civilization. But misfortune seems to have usurped the seat of its tutelary genius, and given it ruin and desolation for its prayers.

CHAPTER IV

COUNTER-EXPEDITIONS OF THE SPANISH, AND THE BEGINNINGS OF TEXAS

Mission San Francisco de los Tejas

THE capture of a French vessel on the coast of Yucatan had given the Spaniards information of La Salle's coming and stimulated them to make some efforts to defeat his plans. The viceroy strengthened the northeastern frontier of Mexico by the establishment of a villa and presidio at Monclova in Coahuila; the one, as judged by prevailing Spanish standards, very populous, and the other unusually formidable. Two hundred and fifty families were sent to the villa, and the garrison numbered two hundred and seventy. During the next three years four expeditions by sea were sent from Vera Cruz to search for the French colony and destroy it. They found the wrecks of two of the ships which had helped to bring it, but St. Louis itself, not lying exactly on the coast, they missed. At the same time a search by land was instituted. By order of the viceroy of New Spain, Governor De Aguayo of Nuevo León sent a company of cavalry under Captain Alonso de León to follow the coast along from Tampico northward and try to find the intruding Frenchmen. This detachment passed the Rio Grande and came to another river, which the Spaniards called the Solo. It widened at its mouth into a lake, which they could not pass, and they returned without news of the French. Another expedition under De León terminated at the same point, and brought back no further information. By this time the impression began to exist in New Spain that the whole story about a French colony on the bay of Espíritu Santo was without foundation ; but there still came reports of white men who were said to be living in that quarter, and by and by an old Frenchman, naked and painted like the savages, was found among them and carried to Mexico. This roused a new interest in the matter, and the viceroy determined to send an expedition which should penetrate to the bay and ascertain the facts. He dispatched, therefore, in the year 1689, eighty men under De León accompanied by a Franciscan padre named Manzanet, who played an important part in the events which followed. This party finally reached Fort St. Louis and found, as has been told already, that the colony had been destroyed by the Indians. The mission of De León was now accomplished ; but plans were soon devised for a fourth expedition, which should leave permanent Spanish establishments in the country, and thus forestall its occupation by the French. The Indians in the vicinity of Fort St. Louis had reported that there was among them a small band of Tejas led by the governor of these Indians and accompanied by four Frenchmen.[1] These Tejas were a long way from home, for their people lived on the upper Neches and the Trinity in what is now known as " East Texas." De León before returning south secured an interview with them and took two of the Frenchmen, who had adopted Indian ways, into custody. But Padre Manzanet, after some encouraging words from the governor of the Tejas in response to his exhortation, promised to come again to his people the next year and bring other priests like himself.

As a result of this expedition there were several meetings of the viceroy and other prominent men in Mexico to devise measures to Christianize the Indians in the country just coming into notice, and keep out the French. De León and Manzanet were sent for and interviewed on the subject by the viceroy. The captain seems to have dwelt on the fact that there was said to be settled among the Tejas a considerable number of Frenchmen, who might be reinforced by their countrymen and do much harm to Spanish interests ; while the padre emphasized the desirability of mission work among the Indians, who had expressed their willingness to receive priests and hear the gospel. It was finally decided to send De León back with one hundred and ten soldiers to destroy the fortifications at St. Louis and make a thorough search for Frenchmen, and with him were to go Manzanet and three other padres as missionaries to the Tejas.

[1] See p. 25.

The expedition started from Coahuila in March, 1690. It arrived duly at the deserted fort, to which Manzanet, as he states with evident satisfaction in his account of the journey, set fire with his own hand. Then the party set out for the country of the Tejas. On the way they recovered from the Indians a young man and a boy who had belonged to La Salle's company, and further along they encountered the governor of the Tejas, who had come out to meet them. They provided him with clothing, as Manzanet puts it, " that his people might see how highly we thought of him." Three days later they entered his village.

Soon after reaching the Tejas the padres began to look for a suitable spot on which to locate a church. During this search they were shown a place which they were told the French had selected for their settlement, and they saw there the bodies of two Frenchmen who had shot each other. By and by they found a satisfactory location, and in three days they had erected a church and a dwelling for the priests. With the celebration of masses, the firing of royal salutes, and the chanting of Te Deums the church and villages were dedicated to the founder of the order to which the padres belonged, and the mission thus established was known by the name of San Francisco de los Tejas. Three padres with three soldiers were left in charge, and De León, Manzanet, and the rest went back the way they had come.

The history of Mission San Francisco de los

Tejas is shorter in time, but hardly less abundant
in misfortune, than that of Fort St. Louis. The
padres founded another small establishment near
by and worked zealously, but their experiences included drought and overflow, ruining the harvests
and followed by famine and pestilence. The Indians refused to live in communities, and the soldiers became unmanageable and outrageous in
their conduct. Finally the viceroy ordered the
abandonment of the mission, and in October, 1693,
the padres and soldiers buried whatever property
they could not carry away with them and departed.
Only one of the Spaniards had died there, but they
had little more real success to boast of than the
French. The mission was revived in 1716 under
the name of San Francisco de los Neches, and in
1730 it was transferred to the San Antonio River,
where it became known as San Francisco de la
Espada.[1]

The exact locality of San Francisco de los Tejas
is now unknown. It was somewhere between the
Trinity and the Neches, probably near the latter,
about forty-five miles in a southwesterly direction
from the present town of Nacogdoches. The
wooden buildings, altogether different from the im-
posing and substantial structures erected further
west, where stone was almost necessarily used and
where the builders had more time for their work,
soon disappeared, and nothing was left to mark
the spot. It might possibly, however, by a careful

[2] See p. 71.

examination of the records and the ground and comparison of the facts, be even yet identified.

In 1691 another expedition was led to the north-eastern frontier by Captain Domingo Terán. It was organized in two divisions, one going by land and the other by sea. The first division consisted of fifty soldiers, nine priests, and a number of attendants, etc.; the second was made up of forty seamen. The purpose of this *entrada* was to strengthen the missions already existing and to establish others, to look for Frenchmen or any foreigners who might be found among the Indians, and to learn as much as possible about the country and the natives. Captain Terán accompanied the division that went by land, and with it was also Padre Manzanet in the capacity of commissary. The history of the expedition is the same old story of mismanagement and misfortune so common in the chronicles of Spanish efforts at colonization. To mischievous dissensions between Terán and Manzanet was added failure to accomplish the junction of the land and the sea divisions until the summer was past, and the whole force did not start from Mission San Francisco de los Tejas for its objective point, the country of the Cadodachos, until near the opening of winter. The destination was reached,[1] but Terán did little in fulfillment of his instructions from the viceroy. Both going and returning his men suffered greatly from cold and hunger, and it was fortunate enough for them that

[1] The expedition penetrated apparently to Red River.

they were allowed to go back home by way of
Espíritu Santo and the Gulf rather than overland.

The attention drawn to the land beyond the Rio
Grande by the establishment of Fort St. Louis
and the resulting Spanish *entradas* gave it at
last a name, Tejas, or, in the usual English form,
Texas.[1] The Indians called by this name had a
considerable degree of civilization and a pretty
well-defined locality. The tribes between it and
the Rio Grande, as it appeared to the Spanish in
their five *entradas*, were insignificant in their
numbers and roving in their habits. Manzanet
remarks that in 1690 De León's company did not
find a single Indian between the Rio Grande and
the land of the Tejas. They had observed no natural feature that had so impressed them as to make
them call the country by its name. There were in
the district they had traversed but two important
localities for which they had specific designations :
Espíritu Santo, and Texas, the country of the Indians among whom the mission had been established. They manifested no desire to repeat the
French experiment of a settlement on the bay, or

[1] The manuscripts vary with little partiality between Tejas and
Texas; but the earliest English books in which the name occurs,
such as Pike's *Expeditions* and the translation known as Hum-
boldt's *New Spain*, use only the form Texas. This has fixed the
spelling of the name as applied to the land ; but the name of the
Indians is usually spelled Tejas. In one or two other Texas names
in the spelling of which the same alternatives once prevailed, the
x has finally triumphed entirely, *e. g.* Bexar and Mexia ; the first
of these two, however, is perhaps better written Béjar for the
period previous to the Revolution.

the State might now be known by a name altogether too sacred for its busy secular habits.   After
the expedition of 1689 there was but one people
in the country it penetrated of whom the Spaniards in Mexico thought seriously, and that was
the Tejas Indians; but one district there, besides
Espíritu Santo, of which they talked, and that was
the country of the same Indians, which they called
Texas.   If the evidence of one of the missionaries
can be accepted, — and there seems no good reason
to the contrary, — Tejas was the name, not of a
single tribe, but of a confederacy of nearly thirty,
including the nine tribes of the Asinais or Cenis.
It was but natural that this name should be extended to the whole region, theretofore without one
of its own.   Nuevas Filipinas, which was for some
time the official designation, was not sufficiently
upon the popular tongue, and was at length displaced entirely by Texas.

CHAPTER V

Expedition of Saint-Denis

THE danger of occupation by the French having disappeared for the time, the Spanish at once relapsed into their customary neglect, and for more than twenty years little attention was given to Texas. The work of founding missions, converting the Indians, and widening the limits of actual Spanish occupation was not entirely suspended; but while the occasion demanded energy and haste, it was answered with the neglect and tardiness of blind security. The most noteworthy outcome of such effort as was made was the establishment, in the year 1700, of the mission of San Juan Bautista near the Rio Grande, which remained for fifteen years the Spanish outpost in the direction of Texas, and which accordingly, when the movement for the occupation of that country was renewed, became a very important centre.

Again the principal explanation of Spanish dilatoriness is to be found in Europe. The aggressions of Louis XIV. caused an organization among the German princes to resist him, and finally led to a war which began with a French invasion of Ger-

many in 1688 and raged fiercely, keeping the whole
of western Europe busy, till the peace of Ryswick
in 1697. The next four years were spent by the
powers in diplomatic chess-play and preparation for
another war which was evidently impending, and
which bade fair to be still bloodier and more prolonged. It came according to expectation, and ful-
filled its worst promises of evil. Its causes were
sufficient, as they must be estimated by the historian
who is experienced in weighing the motives which
produce war ; for the Spanish empire, which hardly
more than a century previous had been the mighti-
est power of Europe, was becoming unable to hold
together and protect itself, and the nations waited
impatiently, France the most eager of all, for the
struggle over the spoils to begin. The death of the
childless king Charles II. in 1700 was the signal
for the outbreak, and the contention was ended only
by the treaties of Utrecht and Baden, concluded
respectively in the years 1713 and 1714.

Leaving out of the question, therefore, the relative inertness and inefficiency of the Spanish as
colonizers, it is not difficult to understand why
Spain did not anticipate France in securing the
mouth of the Mississippi, and why she did not take
firm hold of Texas at once. During the first decade
after the founding of the mission among the Tejas,
she was practically without a king, and during a
large part of the next thirteen years her people
were divided between two rival sovereigns backed,
the one by France, and the other by the allies in

opposition. The eagle, sick and attacked in its own nest, could not fly abroad in search of prey.

France made good use of the interval. She was busy enough at home, it is true ; but her resources had been nursed into a marvelous development by Colbert, and she still had men and supplies to send to America. Had she not been matched, for the moment, against almost the whole of Europe, it is possible that she might have established herself in Louisiana for all time. But the nearer and more glittering prize tempted the ambition of the king of France, and led him to waste his strength in contending for the mastery of the Old World. It was no quixotic folly that led William of Orange to enter on his desperate struggle with Louis XIV. ; for it now looks to the historian as if the work of subverting European liberty, in which Napoleon afterwards failed, was about to be done before his time. But even the farsighted William builded wiser than he knew. Neither he nor Louis could understand that the premature snatch at empire by France was only making opportunity for England, and that the cost of the southern Netherlands and Franche-Comté, and the Bourbon inheritance in Spain, would be the loss of Texas first, and finally of Louisiana, of Canada, and of India.

The peace of Ryswick was hardly more than concluded when France took advantage of the lull in military operations to make good her possession of Louisiana. In 1699 an expedition led by Iberville established a French colony at Old Biloxi,

west of Mobile Bay, and from that time dates the
permanent settlement of the country. In 1718 New
Orleans was founded, and the work which La Salle
had planned, in which he had labored and suffered
with such heroism, and which had finally cost him
his life, was done at length. The French had obtained control of the great river's mouth, and thus,
in some degree, of the vast basin which it drains.
If the results were less than he had hoped, if France
won Louisiana from Spain only to pass it on to
England and the American heirs of England by
and by, this was not his fault; it was simply
because Louis XIV. unconsciously sacrificed an
imperial future in pursuing the phantom of an
imperial present.

France, however, had been none too prompt in
the occupation of Louisiana, for a more energetic
rival than Spain was now contesting for the same
prize. Soon after the settlement had been made
at Old Biloxi, an English ship, one of the three
that had been sent out on the same errand as the
expedition of Iberville, was found by the commandant Bienville in the Mississippi; and its captain
was induced to leave only by being assured that the
French were able to expel him.

The period between the peace of Ryswick and
the beginning of the war of the Spanish Succession
is marked by a complete change in the relations of
the two powers that were now face to face on the
shore of the Gulf of Mexico. Previous to this,
Spain had been, from motives of self-protection and

from the common European interest, an enemy of
France; and La Salle, when seeking to obtain from
Louis XIV. the necessary equipment for his expedition to colonize Louisiana in 1684, had sought
the king's favor for his enterprise by framing
plausible schemes for the conquest of the Spanish
mining province of New Biscay from Louisiana as
a base. But when England, France, and Holland
undertook to dispose of the Spanish inheritance by
a partition treaty, the wounded pride of Charles II.
rejected the arrangement and detached Louis XIV.
from it by bequeathing to his second grandson
the Spanish territory undivided. In the war of the
Spanish Succession, therefore, which followed the
death of Charles II., the sympathies of most of
the people of Spain were with France, and the
formal relations of the French and Spanish colonies in America became peaceful.

Meanwhile, however, the French had done much
towards building up their new colony. The life of
their settlements depended in large measure on their
trade with the Indians, and this trade they wisely
sought to attract and foster by all possible means.
Finally, in 1712, Louis XIV. granted a monopoly
of the Louisiana trade to Antoine Crozat for fifteen
years, and the event was followed by the inaugura-
tion of a commercial activity in that colony that
became the occasion of a new turn in the history of
Texas. It was, of course, not difficult for an alert
man of business like Crozat to see that much would
be gained by adding a trade with the neighboring

Spanish colonies to that with the Indians, and to this end his policy was directed. His plans were furthered and his work greatly facilitated by the active coöperation of Governor Lamothe Cadillac, the official representative of the home government and special trustee of its interests in Louisiana, who became by his action in this case, as the sequel will show, the agent in delivering possession of Texas to the Spanish.

In 1713 Cadillac, in accordance with the desire of Crozat, sent a ship to Vera Cruz for the purpose of opening a trade with Mexico; but even the improved diplomatic relations of France and Spain could hardly be expected to admit of the growth of a direct commerce between their colonies. Spain especially was exceedingly jealous of her monopoly of her American colonial trade. Consent to any treaty stipulation in breach of it had to be wrung from her by war, and was given in much the same spirit in which she would have surrendered a conquered province. The viceroy rejected all the overtures of Cadillac, and the expedition was fruitless.

The opportunity desired by Crozat and Cadillac now appeared in another quarter. Fray Francisco Hidalgo, who had worked at the short-lived mission of San Francisco de los Tejas, and had afterwards helped to establish that of San Juan Bautista near the Rio Grande, had still later returned to the scene of his earlier labors in Texas, and had remained for several years as a missionary among the Asinais.

During this time he and his co-workers of San Juan Bautista had been constant in their appeals to the viceroy to reoccupy the country of the Tejas, abandoned by the friars in 1693, where Padre Hidalgo himself was doing such effective work for Catholicism and for Spain by teaching the Indians and winning a secure influence over them, against the day of threatened French encroachment. But it was impossible to inspire the authorities in Mexico with the enthusiasm of the Franciscans, and after long and impatient waiting, Hidalgo, like Cadillac, laid aside his patriotism for the moment, and in his excess of religious zeal appealed for help to the French. Early in 1711 he wrote a letter to the governor of Louisiana inviting his coöperation in the establishment of a mission among the Asinais. In the course of time the letter was received by Cadillac, and the invitation was responded to with a promptness in sharp contrast with the Spanish neglect. The details of Hidalgo's proposition are not known, but it involved in some way the suggestion of an experiment at an intercolonial trade to be carried on through Texas, of which the governor was quick to take advantage. He sent out a French expedition, whose general object was evidently to try such an experiment. How far the results that followed were foreseen it is not easy to say; for the plan was largely clandestine, and the statements contained in the documents as to the purposes of the expedition are evidently not frank. It may be that all was anticipated substantially as

it happened — that Hidalgo was willing to let the
French enjoy even an illicit commerce with Mexico,
if that would facilitate his mission work among the
Indians, and that Cadillac was indifferent to the
Spanish possession of Texas if a chain of settlements could be made through which trade might
pass from the Red River to the Rio Grande. If
these were their respective views, then neither could
have been greatly surprised or disappointed by the
outcome.

The leader chosen for the expedition was Louis
Juchereau de Saint-Denis.[1] He was doubtless the
best available man for the place. He had previously led parties into Texas, knew both the Spanish language and that of the Indians, and was
experienced in dealing with the natives. Already
he had played a more important part in extending
the French explorations and settlement on the
western border of Louisiana than any other man
in the colony. Early in the spring of 1700 he had
accompanied Bienville up Red River to the village
of the Yatase Indians, where they heard from some
visiting Caddos a report of the existence of a Spanish settlement five days' journey towards the west.
The records, however, furnish no other evidence of
any such settlement in Texas at the time. About
two months later Saint-Denis ascended the river
again, passing through the country of the Natchitoches, and reaching finally that of the Caddos.

[1] This Saint-Denis must be carefully distinguished from his
older brother, who worked mainly in the Ohio valley.

Here the Indians told him that they had seen no Spanish for more than two years. About 1705, if his own statement to the Mexican authorities is not misunderstood, he must have crossed Texas to the Rio Grande, but of the details of the expedition nothing is known. So, when the call from Cadillac came to him in 1713, he doubtless felt that the enterprise that was to be committed to his charge was one for which he had already paved the way.

Previous to starting on the expedition Saint-Denis made an agreement with Cadillac, and obtained from him a passport. The two instruments taken together, the latter being read between the lines, indicate clearly enough the real nature of the work that Saint-Denis had undertaken. He agreed to carry goods to the value of ten thousand livres out of the stock of Crozat and try to dispose of them in Mexico. His passport stated that he was to take twenty-four men and as many Indians as needed, to search for the mission of Hidalgo, and there to buy horses and cattle for the Louisiana colony.

The expedition started from Mobile in the late summer or the early fall of 1713, but was delayed several months at Biloxi, and probably did not enter Texas until some time in 1714. It consisted of five canoes, laden with men and goods, and the route was up the Mississippi and the Red River to the country of the Natchitoches, and thence west to that of the Asinais. At the village of the Natchitoches where the overland march began, Saint-

Denis stored the goods and left ten men to guard them. Then, adding thirty Natchitoches Indians to his force, he proceeded to the Asinais, where he spent six months trading with the Indians, taking horses, cattle, and buffalo hides in exchange for guns, beads, knives, and cloth. During this period he made a trip back to the Natchez to report to Cadillac and bring more goods.

Unconsciously the Asinais lent themselves as instruments to Saint-Denis's policy. He found among them well-marked traces of Hidalgo's work, and the Indians were anxious to have the zealous padre among them again. Their desires concurred, at least in some degree, with the aims of Saint-Denis; so, when they besought him to ask the missionaries, and especially Hidalgo, to come back to them, he took their governor and twenty-five men to act as guides, and set out towards the Rio Grande, apparently to do as they wished. After six weeks' marching, in the course of which the party fought and defeated a band of Indians hostile to the Asinais, they arrived at the presidio of the Rio Grande, or the mission of San Juan Bautista, two leagues from the river on the Mexican side, and some thirty-five miles below the site of the present Eagle Pass.

How far the real objects of the expedition were stated to the commander of the presidio, Captain Diego Ramón, or to what extent he penetrated the designs of Saint-Denis, is not clear. His action was such as would seem to have been wisest in any case.

He treated the Frenchmen well, but detained them until he could get instructions to fit the case from the viceroy.

Meanwhile Saint-Denis contrived to send a letter to Cadillac informing him of the state of affairs, expressing confidence as to the outcome, and indicating the writer's hope that his services in connection with the enterprise would secure him the patronage of the governor. And for the tedium and suspense of waiting for the viceroy's answer, he found relief in the company of the granddaughter of Captain Diego Ramón, to whom he soon became engaged. Before he returned finally to Louisiana they were married; and some historians, in dealing with this episode of the expedition of Saint-Denis, have so far lost the perspective that they have allowed the real significance of his work to be obscured by the incidental romance.

By and by a guard from Coahuila was sent to conduct Saint-Denis to the city of Mexico. Even before the news from the presidio of the Rio Grande had reached the viceroy, he had heard from the Spanish at Pensacola of the coming of the expedition. But there were evidently private suggestions that the *entrada* was in no spirit of hostility to the Spanish interests, or at any rate that Saint-Denis himself had no such motive. The representative of the outraged majesty of Spain did not fling the French adventurer into a dungeon, as might have been expected, but simply questioned him closely as to his objects and requested him to

make a written statement of them. This was given
to Espinosa, the fiscal, in order that he might report
thereon to a council which was held soon after to
consider it.

Though Saint-Denis had told, in his *declaración*,
less than half the truth, it contained enough to set
the Spaniards thinking. Espinosa saw and set
forth clearly in his report the danger in the situation. They were threatened with French encroachment, the loss of the northern trade, and the discovery of their precious mines. To prevent all
this, he recommended that the governors of the exposed provinces be directed to keep out the French,
and that the missions in that quarter be reëstablished. The council, in accordance with his
report, planned an expedition to establish four
missions among the Tejas Indians. Thenceforth
the French were to be more strictly watched, and
any attempt at encroachment reported promptly.

The expedition was organized under the leadership of Captain Domingo Ramón, son of the governor of the presidio. The strength of it was, to
all appearances, contemptibly inadequate for the
work in hand. Besides Ramón, his son Diego, and
Saint-Denis, of whose place in the company I shall
have more to say presently, there were only twenty-
two soldiers. This little force would hardly have
been regarded as sufficient to secure the defense
of such a distant and exposed frontier if there had
been any reason to expect hostility on the part of
those against whom the barrier was to be erected.

The party included twelve friars, besides three lay brothers, and a number of civilians. In all there were sixty-five. It is worth noting, however, that there were a few families and several married men whose wives had come with them. Small as the colony was, it was better suited for permanence than any the Spanish had previously sent into the northeastern wilds.

An interesting fact, and one not entirely explicable from the records, is that Saint-Denis accompanied the expedition as an important salaried official. The contemporary accounts do not speak with one voice as to his duties. They call him now *cabo comboyador* (chief of convoy) and again *conductor de víveres* (quartermaster); possibly he performed both functions. In any case, it seems that he was quite helpful to the Spanish; and one can scarcely doubt that he was regarded as a sort of personal pledge of French acquiescence in their designs. It is, however, difficult to acquit him of double-dealing. On at least two occasions while he was seeking to ingratiate himself with the Spanish and induce them to undertake the reoccupation of Texas, once while he was at Presidio del Rio Grande, and again when he was in the city of Mexico, he contrived to send to Governor Cadillac information as to the course of his affairs; and in the latter case he gave warning of the expected Spanish *entrada* and proposed a counter-expedition to Espíritu Santo Bay. And while in his statement to the viceroy he enlarged on the desirability of fixing the boundary between the French and the Spanish at the Mississippi, in his letter to Cadillac from Mexico he favored placing it at the Rio Grande.

In January, 1716, Cadillac wrote that he had information from Saint-Denis in Mexico of the intention of the Spanish to make a settlement among the Natchitoches, and that he would instruct him to oppose it, because that country belonged to the French king; he did not, however, indicate his plan in case they confined themselves, as in fact they did, to the valley of the Sabine. In 1721 Bienville declared, in a protest against the Spanish settlement at Adaes, that when he gave permission to the missionaries to establish themselves there it was with the assurance from them that they meant only to found a mission and preach the gospel. This is no doubt true, and it is possible that the assurance was suggested by Saint-Denis himself. It indicates that Bienville, who was keenly alive to the interests of France, saw no danger to those interests in having Spanish settlements so near the border if they were purely missions; but it is difficult to see how he could entertain such views. And as for Saint-Denis, to acquit him of treachery to France on that supposition is impossible. He was too evidently moved by other considerations.

Considerable light on the real nature of Saint-Denis's designs and on the relations that existed subsequently between the French and Spanish along the Texas border, and between the missionaries and

the Spanish officials, is reflected backward by some
correspondence that took place in the year 1719
between Bénard de la Harpe, who had just established a French post among the Nassonites on Red
River above Natchitoches, and Padre Margil,[1] superior of the Texas missions. La Harpe wrote a most
cordial letter to the good father, professing great
reverence for him, and an earnest desire that they
should maintain perfect harmony which should be
useful in upbuilding the missions. He went on to
say that he knew that supplies were necessary in
order to preach the gospel, and that he would suggest a sure way of getting them. Margil had only
to write to his friends in New Mexico, Parral, and
Nuevo León that they could find among the Natchitoches or Nassonites all sorts of European merchandise at reasonable prices, on which they could make
sure profit. La Harpe would fix prices with them
and give Margil five per cent. of sales. He urged
this as an effective means of opening trade, of serving many persons who needed the goods, and of
establishing the missions securely ; and he averred
that the offer came from a heart devoted to his reverence, in which benevolence had a larger place
than any other motive. Finally he begged for ten
cows and two bulls, praying that Margil would send
to him for a supply of maize and beans in return,
and remarked that he had sent by the bearer a
present for the padre, consisting of ten pieces of
Brittany linen and one piece of damask.

[1] In the French documents the name is written " Marsillo," but
it evidently should be Margil.

By the same bearer La Harpe sent a brief, though courteous, communication to Governor Alarcón, transmitting a diplomatic note from Bienville, but not mentioning trade. Soon afterwards the bearer returned with answers to both letters. The governor's reply was short and direct. While acknowledging the orders of his king and his own desire to keep on good terms with the French, he expressed surprise at their having settled among the Nassonites on territory belonging to Spain, and suggested that he might have to force them to withdraw.

But Margil wrote in a very different tone. He said that he had heard of the arrival of La Harpe among the Nassonites and wished to know him, and that he should prize his friendship and seek to merit it. He accepted with joy the proposal of harmony. He said he would write to his friends as La Harpe had suggested ; but, as it was not fitting for a religious to engage in trade, their correspondence would best be secret, not only for fear of possible consequences, but because they were not friends with Alarcón, and he might foil their purposes. He did not think, however, that Alarcón would stay long in the province. There were many complaints against him ; for example, he had not executed the viceroy's orders, nor had he dealt properly with the Indians. Margil promised to keep La Harpe well posted, and said that when the streams fell he would send him four cows and a bull, which were all he could spare just then.

After this specimen of the intrigues that were being hatched in the frontier nest, in evident continuance of the policy of Saint-Denis, there needs no further illustration of the work in which he was engaged.

The expedition led by Ramón made its final start from the Rio Grande just beyond the presidio of that name, April 27, 1716, following the route previously traveled by Saint-Denis, which became, under the name of the Old San Antonio or Presidio Road, the first great Texas highway. After a march of about two months the Spanish reached the country of the Tejas, who received them with great friendliness. Mission San Francisco was reestablished, but on a site about four leagues farther inland than where it first stood. Instead, however, of the original designation "de los Tejas," it was rechristened "de los Neches."[1] Besides this, five other missions were founded, whose names were as follows: Nuestra Señora de la Guadalupe, La Purísima Concepción, San Joseph, San Miguel de Linares, and Nuestra Señora de los Dolores. They were to serve respectively, in the order in which they have been named, beginning with San Francisco, the Neches, or the Nacogdoches, the Asinais, the Noaches, the Adaes, and the Aes. Guadalupe was in the neighborhood of the present town of Nacogdoches, and the others were situated in an irregular group around it at distances ranging

---

[1] It served several Indian tribes, and the designation varies to some extent.

from twenty-five to fifty miles, the last two being
well towards the east and near the French settlements already established on Red River.

This mission founding was not completed until
in the year 1717. In the mean time Ramón had
paid a friendly visit to the French post among the
Natchitoches, and Saint-Denis had gone to Mobile.
As to the subsequent operations of the latter, the
accounts differ greatly, and it is a curious commen-
tary on the inner history of this episode that the
Spanish documents make a much more favorable
showing for him than the French. It seems, in
fact, that his conduct was better understood in
Louisiana than in Mexico, except perhaps by the
Ramón family and some of the padres. Aside from
the conflict in the sources, it is evident that, while
he gave out that he was going to Mobile to settle
up his affairs and move to Mexico to serve the Spanish, his real purpose was to organize the illicit trade
at which he had been aiming from the start. The
risks of his enterprise were plain, and he could get
none of Crozat's goods until a colonial company was
formed to help it on. Then he went back with the
merchandise, representing it as his own. The effect
was to rouse suspicion against him in Mexico. The
goods were seized, and he was imprisoned. After
a short time he was released by a royal order, but
it provided that he and his wife should be sent to
Guatemala. Soon afterwards he escaped to Louisiana and reëntered the French service, and in the
course of time his wife rejoined him.

His work had been effective in everything but the results he wished. Like a good vassal in old feudal days, he served his immediate lords, Cadillac and Crozat, better than he served his king; and it is probable that if the government of either France or Spain had really understood what he was about, he would have been rewarded with a halter.

But Spain owed him much; for he had given it possession of a goodly land. Thenceforth, until the Anglo-Americans came, Texas followed the fortunes of Mexico.

CHAPTER VI

THE Spanish have inherited the imperial, and perhaps also a sufficient degree of the colonizing, instinct; but the empire they built has been lost to them by reason of their ineffective work in colonization. This is at least the proximate cause. It may be doubted, indeed, whether the native strength of the Peninsula was ever adequate for a struggle over world-wide dominance; but if it were, the national experience of the Spaniard never gave it proper direction till it had suffered a virtual paralysis. The Spanish explorers were daring, energetic, and persistent enough for any undertaking. No adventurers went farther or risked and suffered more. In the annals of the discovery and conquest of America, the wanderings of Cabeza de Vaca, Coronado, and De Soto stand forth preëminent, as much for hardihood as fruitlessness. But the *conquistador* was not backed up by the settler, and the officials could not organize a compact political and social system from native material alone. So it was that, while the explorations and claims of the Spanish were wide enough for a schoolboy's dream, their grasp was too weak for permanence.

The ultimate explanation of this lies at least partly in the religious history of Spain. The English colonies were peopled to a large extent by those who, much as they loved England, preferred the hardships of America to conformity at home. The domestic quarrels, therefore, of the English served at least to secure their possessions abroad. But religious uniformity in Spain, purchased at the cost of the expulsion of the Moors and Jews and the extirpation of heresy, left no such popular motive to emigration ; and, had it been otherwise, the Spanish heretic would have been excluded from the settlements of his countrymen in America, just as the Huguenot was from those of France. Considering these facts together with that already noted, — that all the failing strength of Spain was required to maintain its rights and claims in Europe, — it is not strange that the policy of that government seemed so weak in meeting the crises in the history of its colonies.

The Spanish settlements in Texas were of three types : the ecclesiastical, the military, and the civil, named respectively the mission, the presidio, and the pueblo or *población*. Before going any farther, these must be briefly described.

The mission was the instrument for accomplishing one of the main objects professed — and no doubt sincerely — by the Spanish in their colonizing work in America, *i. e.* the Christianizing of the Indians. Its principal element was a group of priests, usually quite small and sometimes includ-

ing one or more lay brethren, whose duty it was to
instruct the natives at the same time in the elements
of Christianity and of civilization, or, as Eden's
translation of the bull of Pope Alexander VI. dividing the New World puts it, " in the Catholyke
fayth and good maners." The instruction in the
one case was largely in the forms of the Catholic
religion, and in the other mainly in agriculture and
the commonest industries and arts. In order to
accomplish these purposes it was necessary to induce the Indians to abandon their roving life and
settle in reach of the padres. A natural adjunct of
the mission, therefore, was the pueblo, or village
of the natives. Those who could be induced to accept the mission-village life were known as *Indios
reducidos*, in distinction from the hostile rovers,
who were called *Indios bravos*. The most effective
means of " reducing " the Indians lay in the gifts
that were distributed among them from time to
time; but, as might be supposed, the "reduction "
was in most cases only temporary. The census reports made periodically from the various missions
show clearly how shifting was the population held
together by such means. By Spanish law the Indians could be detained in the pueblos by force,
and the policy of the missionaries was to prevent
their escape if possible, and, when they ran away in
spite of priestly vigilance, to recapture them; but
the authorities would not always furnish the necessary soldiers.

The best idea of the mission and its actual daily

round of life may be had from the detailed contemporary accounts that have been left us. The following description of the village connected with La Concepción at San Antonio and of the common life at the missions is translated from a report of the missionaries on the state of the missions in 1762:

The pueblo is composed of two rows of stone houses and huts in which the Indians live, which are furnished with boilers, flat earthen pans, pots, and other domestic utensils, the pueblo being also surrounded by a wall for its protection and defense. It has its inclosed fields, the necessary supplies of water, a flowing irrigation ditch with its stone dam, and a ranch with its dwellings for the families who look after its two hundred mares, one hundred and ten horses, six hundred and ten head of cattle, and twenty-two hundred head of goats and sheep. There are stored in its granary, which is a single large room, about eight hundred *fanegas* [1] of corn and fifty of beans for the supply of the pueblo.

The same report describes the management of the Indians at the missions as follows: —

The catechism of the Gentile and Christian Indians is uniform in all the missions, and the same which the reverend father founders, highly venerable for their virtues and character, used. . . .

Every day all the Indians recite in concert the text of the Christian doctrine according to the catechism of Ripalda, in the morning before work and in the evening after it. Three or four times a week the ministers instruct their Indians, with reference to the same text of

[1] A *fanega* is about one hundred pounds.

the catechism, in the mysteries of our holy faith and the obligations of Christians, with similes and arguments adapted to their inexpressible rusticity.

The Gentiles are taught separately by means of their interpreters, which requires extra expenditure of time, until they are grounded in the elements; and when they have shown some disposition to remain at the missions (which not even the oldest Christians have in full measure) holy baptism is administered to them. Besides the recitation in concert, the boys are also instructed separately every day by their fiscal, and often by their ministers, in order to see their progress.

To the dying and the sick is promptly administered holy baptism, if they are infidels, and to the Christians are administered the holy sacraments of penance, the eucharist, and extreme unction . . .

For those who come from the woods married, the natural contract is ratified (leaving only one wife to those who bring several) before their baptism, and the Christians are married at the proper time by the church officials and in conformity with the regulations of the holy Council of Trent.

All those who are of sufficient age confess and receive the sacrament, according to their respective ability to understand, during Lent and on any festivals when they wish. . . .

The missionaries have paid special attention to the temporal assistance of the Indians, both because this is their personal business, and because it is one of the most important means of subsistence for those who live at the missions, and for the attraction of those who inhabit the woods, who observe and consider the advantages the others enjoy.

For this purpose are used the cattle which the missionaries manage to acquire in order to kill, at each mission every Sunday and on some special feast days, four or five head, according to the number of people — dividing them into pieces in order that each individual may have his corresponding ration; and mutton is given to those who are sick.

The corn crop is consumed by giving the Indians what they need for all purposes; and they are also furnished beans, pumpkins, watermelons, melons, pepper, salt, and sugar, which is made from cane that they take care to plant at each mission annually, because this is the best thing to regale the Indians and the most pleasing to their appetite. In the missions cotton and wool are used by making them into *mantas*,[1] *terlingas*,[2] *rebozos*,[3] coarse cloths, and blankets for their protection and covering.

The surplus of all these products, if they are produced in abundance and there are persons to buy them, is sold for secured bills, which are sent to our reverend father guardian, whence they pass to our brother syndic, in order that they may be laid out in cloths, flannels, hats, knives, boilers, pots, flat earthen pans, *metates*,[4] tobacco, glass beads, *rechas*,[5] hatchets, crowbars, pickaxes, bridles, thread, needles, saddles, and whatever is necessary, and for the goods to satisfy the Spanish stewards and serving men for the care of the mission, crops, and cattle.

[1] Shawls or light bed coverings of cotton or wool.

[2] What this word means, I am unable to say. It is probably a copyist's corruption. I have not been able to find the original report. — G. P. G.

[3] Light scarfs used to throw over the head.

[4] Flat stones on which boiled maize is crushed into a pulp.

[5] Probably meant for *rejas*, ploughshares.

For the same purpose, in large part, is used also, by direction of our sacred college, the annual offering which the king our lord contributes for the missionaries, our prelates assisting us with chocolate, powder, cloth, under-clothes, drugs, and what is, from the standpoint of the religious, considered indispensable.

All the aforesaid, with the bills that are taken in (which bills, however, are not always obtained), is spent for ornaments, vases, sacred images, and other necessaries for divine worship, adornment of the churches, and sat-isfaction of the workmen. It is used also in dressing, adorning, and maintaining men, women, and children, not only by annual appropriations, but on all occasions when they tear, lose, or waste the clothing.

The horses are used in looking after the cattle, gather-ing the flocks, and in other services of the missions to which they belong; most of them being lost or stolen, either by enemies or by the Indians of the missions them-selves when they escape.

The Indians are assisted, when they are sick, with medicines which this country furnishes, and some which are brought in for the purpose. They are visited by the fathers and by other persons who have been charged with the care of them; and in serious cases they are fed from the kitchen of the fathers, and in all they are re-lieved from work. For this reason not a few of them get to making pretenses, and the missionaries, in order to keep them from running away, behave as if they were deceived by them.

The labor of the Indians is to plant the fields, look after the cattle, to water the crops, to clear away weeds, and to gather their grain, to erect their dwellings, and other buildings of the missions to which the community attends; but with such slowness and carelessness that it is always necessary for some Spaniard to be directing them, and four of them are not sufficient for what could be done by one. They work, with a lack of energy corresponding to their inborn laziness, some at weaving and in the forges, and others as carpenters and bricklayers, in which trades instruction has been furnished them by the missionaries with no small endeavor for their comfort. They have been provided also with the proper tools for all these occupations.

The employment of the women and children is to spin with *malacates*,[1] and to comb cotton. All this labor constitutes no impediment to their spiritual welfare or the help due their families, but is very moderate and conformable to their want of culture, little talent, and great sloth.

Naturally enough recruits for the mission work were obtained among the friars rather than the secular clergy, and that in Texas was done by Franciscans, who came either from Querétaro or from Zacatecas. The colleges of the order at these two places were, therefore, the bases from which the efforts of the missionaries were organized and directed. The Querétarans and Zacatecans worked separately, but, while exhibiting perhaps a touch of jealousy now and then, usually in all harmony.

The presidio was the fort, or instrument of military occupation. It was used where defense or protection with arms was a necessity. There was generally at least one for each group of exposed

---

[1] Rough spindles.

missions, so located as to be most effective in sheltering them all. It was not uncommon for a little guard of soldiers to be stationed at a mission, if there were no presidio immediately at hand, but the padres usually preferred to be without them; for the soldiers sent to do duty as *presidiales*, or mission guards, were of the lowest type of humanity that could be picked up, and their outrages on the Indians often interfered seriously with the work the missionaries had been sent to do.

The noblest and most enduring visible monuments of the Spanish occupation are the mission and presidio buildings. Those erected in east Texas were the oldest; but owing to the abundance of wood and lack of stone in that country most of them were built of perishable materials, and they have long since disappeared so completely that no one knows even where they stood. There was till recently one notable exception in the old Stone Fort at Nacogdoches, erected for the defense of the pueblo of Bucareli, which was moved thither from the banks of the Trinity about 1778; but that has recently been torn down to make room for a business house.[1] In the west, however, timber was less abundant and stone plentiful, and the mission buildings in that quarter were massive and endur-

[1] This fort played an important part in the Fredonian war and the disturbances of 1832. It was the last monument of the original Texas, and there is now left perhaps no visible mark by which the old district could be located. The stones have been saved, and it is hoped that the building will be restored some day on a spot suitable for the purpose.

ing. There is an especially interesting group in the ruins of the five missions that were located in and near the city of San Antonio. What means and appurtenances the devotion of the Spanish missionaries and secular authorities led them to provide for the worship of God, even in the wilderness, may be seen from a description of the church of Concepción in the report of 1762, already mentioned. The writer dwells with evident pride on the attractive architecture of the building, the mural decorations, the finely sculptured images of stone, the elegant service for the mass, the supply of ornaments, the rich vestments for the priests, and the convenient and comfortable construction and furnishing of their *vivienda* or dwelling.

The third instrument used by the Spanish in their colonizing work in Texas was the civil settlement. This form was so connected, and often so blended, with the other two, that it is rather difficult to define in general. The Spanish word for any aggregation of settlers is pueblo or *población*. If the settlement acquired special rights of self-government it might still be known by either of these designations, but more specifically it then became a villa or a *ciudad* (city).[1] Its local government was administered by a council known as the *cabildo* or *ayuntamiento*, composed of *alcaldes* (judges), *regidores* (town councilors), and cer-

[1] Under the Mexican government the villas of Texas were the administrative centres or capitals of districts which were known as municipalities. At the time of the Revolution of 1836 these municipalities became the counties of the Republic.

tain other officials. The members were nominally
elected, but the election meant little. The council
had really none of the independence and legislative
power that is possessed by municipal authorities in
the United States. In its more elementary and
theoretical aspects the system of government for
the Spanish colonies in America was quite simple.
They were governed, even to the minutest details
of lawmaking, by the king through a body of his
appointees known as the Council of the Indies.
There were subordinate courts, but no legislative
bodies. Practically, however, there was great confusion. The viceroys had all the power of the king
except as they were expressly limited. The laws
did not harmonize, and the special rights of the
privileged classes and the multitude of conflicting
jurisdictions made all pretense at justice a mockery.
The disorder reached its height towards the early
days of the nineteenth century. The northern provinces were then under a general commandant with
headquarters at Chihuahua. Original judgments
which were given at that time by the provincial
governors were subject to review, if on military
subjects, by the commandant at Chihuahua; if on
fiscal, by the intendant at San Luis Potosí; if on
ecclesiastical, by the bishop at Nuevo León; and
if on civil, by the *audiencia* of Nueva Galicia.

Under such a system local self-government was
only a pretense. Of organized and self-conscious
municipal life expressing itself through popular
elections or mass meetings or any of the recognized

instruments of local public opinion in countries which have inherited English institutions, there was nothing. Neither was there any scope for independent action on the part of the councils. All they could do was to move in prescribed lines. Everything depended ultimately on the decision of authorities who were far away and tardy with their answers. Any attempt to enforce rights by law was like a shot at the moon ; it might be started in the proper direction, but there was little prospect of reaching the mark. The main hope of the settlers was in the forgetfulness or neglect of the distant lawmakers and judges, too ignorant of actual conditions in Texas to rule it wisely, which left them to fight out their own petty quarrels among themselves. Accordingly the minutes of the *cabildos* or *ayuntamientos* are a record of petitions and trivial discussions, which derive their interest from the light they throw on current questions of real importance. They are concerned with grievances of one member of the council against another, with complaints against the neighboring missionaries and *presidiales*, and with other affairs of like weight and import. In 1735 the council of the villa of San Fernando at San Antonio petitioned for a leave of absence for an official who wished to go to Saltillo for medical treatment, contrary to restrictions previously laid on the Canary Island settlers of the villa. The petition was sent to the governor and forwarded with his recommendation in the premises to the viceroy, and the next year the answer came.

The man might go, — presumably he was still alive,
— but he must be watched and if he tried to run
away arrested for a traitor. This is a sufficient
illustration of the nature of municipal government
in Spanish Texas.

One hopeful aspect of the municipal activity
of that period consists in the efforts made at San
Fernando to establish and foster a school system.
These began May 1, 1789, — a date significant
enough, — and continued in a weak and fluttering
way, but evidently gathering strength, up to the
eve of the Revolution in 1835. Inadequate as they
were, they show that the Spanish inhabitants of
Texas were not wholly without noble aspirations ;
and when recounted in connection with the famous
indictment in the Texas declaration of independence
against the Mexican government for its neglect of
popular education, they acquire no small degree of
interest.

But however little of political virility and promise there may have been in the Spanish civil colony, it was the real germ of the typical Peninsular
civilization, and the one which could best be relied
on for successful transplanting to New Spain.
Whether the Spanish appreciated its importance or
not, one secret of their failure lies in the expenditure of energy on the two other colonial types to
the neglect of this. While upwards of twenty-five
missions and presidios were founded first and last
on Texas soil, there were, when the Anglo-Americans began to pour in, but three centres of Spanish

population between the Sabine and the Rio Grande : San Antonio,[1] Goliad,[2] and Nacogdoches. In the rapidity with which settlements began to multiply and spread from that time on, there is a most instructive contrast.

[1] Or Béjar. [2] Or La Bahía.

CHAPTER VII

THE BEGINNINGS OF SAN ANTONIO

As I have said, there were but three permanent
Spanish settlements established in Texas. This, of
course, does not include the old town of Ysleta,
which has always been Indian and not Spanish.
Nor was it a part of the Texas with which we are
now dealing. Although the determination of
boundaries has left it finally within the State, and
the building of the Texas Pacific and Southern
Pacific railways and the growth of El Paso near
by have helped on its real geographical incorporation with the developing commonwealth, it was
completely isolated from the province by the
intervening desert and the fierce Apaches and
Comanches.

Of the three which are properly included, and
which have already been named, San Antonio was
the most important. It was the capital of Texas
during nearly the whole period of Spanish and
Mexican rule.[1] Its situation as outpost in relation
to the Anglo-American colonies caused it to become
the scene of the most desperate fighting in the campaigns of 1835 and 1836 including the defense of

[1] Adaes on the eastern border of the province enjoyed the distinction for a brief season.

the Alamo, the superlatively dramatic episode of all the history of America. It remains the most interesting city in Texas, if not, indeed, in the whole Southwest. In and around it are to be seen the ruins of five notable missions, and in spite of its modern and progressive aspects there is much to remind one of what it has been. Not on account of these facts, however, is a sketch of its beginnings demanded here, but because its settlement was one of the most important features of the making of Texas.

It will be well to brush away at the outset the tissue of legends concerning the origin of San Antonio, which date it back into the last decade of the seventeenth century. They are without the support of any trustworthy evidence. The settlement was begun in 1718, but the accounts of the Saint-Denis expedition contain some interesting references to what was doubtless the site of it. One of these is to the effect that when Saint-Denis and his companions were on their way from the country of the Asinais to the Presidio del Rio Grande, they crossed the San Antonio River at an Indian village, and he remarked the fitness of the place for a presidio. Another, speaking in less uncertain terms, says that, when the party led to the Tejas country by Captain Domingo Ramón in 1716 was marching inward, it encamped on one occasion at some springs to which was given the name San Pedro, and Captain Ramón observed that it was a good place to build a city. The presidio was there within two years, but the city did not come for about a dozen more.

The early history of San Antonio is a study having special interest and attraction on account of the peculiar nature of the settlement. Almost from its founding it was a combination of presidio, mission, and villa, the mission having the usual pueblo. Or perhaps it would better be called an aggregation of the three; for they were not really combined, but there were, of course, necessarily close relations among them. That they did not always get on well together is evident enough from the facts stated in the previous chapter.[1] The settlements at Nacogdoches and Goliad also contained at different times all these three elements, but they do not present so perfect a case of the parallel development of the three in juxtaposition.

At San Antonio the presidio and the mission came together. After the establishment of the eastern group of missions in 1716–17, as the outcome of the Saint-Denis expedition, Commandant Ramón and the padres kept calling for more settlers, until finally the call was answered by Martin de Alarcón, who had been appointed governor of Coahuila, and later of Texas also, that he might look after its colonization. He had been directed to take fifty soldiers, a number of carpenters, blacksmiths, and masons, and some cattle and supplies and push on the work of settlement in Texas. The artisans were to have annual salaries. The purpose

[1] See p. 64.

in bringing them, as expressed in the documents relative to the period, was to instruct the Indians and insure the settlement of the country. Alarcón entered the province and set himself to his task early in 1718. He founded the presidio of San Antonio de Béjar on the San Antonio River, probably near the Indian village whose favorable situation had been noted by Saint-Denis. At the same time he established under the shelter of the presidio the mission of San Antonio de Valero in charge of Padre Olivares. This foundation is scarcely to be regarded as a new mission, but rather as a transfer of the one named San Francisco Solano on the Rio Grande, which Olivares had assisted in founding in the year 1700, and at which he had subsequently worked. The Rio Grande mission was now abandoned, and the Indians were moved — at least so far as it could be effected — to the new establishment on the San Antonio.

The mission of San Antonio de Valero was soon reënforced by several others. In 1720 the mission of San José de Aguayo was founded near by, and in 1722 that of San Xavier de Náxera. In 1729 the presidio of Texas, the defense of the three missions controlled by the Franciscans of Querétaro in the eastern group,[1] was abandoned, and in 1731 these missions were transferred to the less exposed location at San Antonio. Their names before the removal were San Francisco de los Neches, La Purísima Concepción de los Asinais, and San Joseph de

[1] See p. 86.

los Nazones; but the facts that there was already one San José at Béjar and that their distinctive appellations, which were those of the Indian tribes they had served, were no longer applicable, caused the change of the three names respectively to San Francisco de la Espada, La Purísima Concepción de Acuña, and San Juan Capistrano. In this connection it should be remembered that San Francisco de los Neches was the reëstablished San Francisco de los Tejas, and that its history, therefore, dates back to the very beginnings of Texas.

What is now known as the Alamo stands fronting on the Alamo Plaza in one of the busiest parts of the modern city. It is said to have been begun in 1744. It appears to have been the chapel of Mission San Antonio de Valero. The ruins as they now exist cover only a small part of the grounds of the original mission. That the name Alamo, which was applied to the whole group of buildings, superseded the regular ecclesiastical designation was doubtless due to their occupation by a company of Mexican troops known as that of the Alamo of Parras.[1]

To the military and ecclesiastical establishments already fixed between the San Antonio and the San Pedro was added in 1731 a civil settlement known as the villa of San Fernando. This measure had been recommended by the Marqués de Aguayo.

[1] The word *álamo* is Spanish for cottonwood, and a popular but mistaken explanation of the name of the building attributes it to the number of cottonwood trees that once stood near by.

The necessary colonists were obtained mainly from the Canary Islands. A royal decree of 1722 had provided that four hundred families from the Canaries should be brought to Texas as settlers, but none had come ; so another decree issued early in 1729 directed that every vessel leaving the islands for Havana should bring ten or twelve families to be sent to Texas. The next year fifteen or sixteen families, comprising fifty odd persons in all, were actually brought over. Instead, however, of having them transported from Havana to Texas by the comparatively direct and easy route via Espíritu Santo, they were sent in by way of Vera Cruz, and had to make the wearisome march overland from Guantitlan, near the city of Mexico, to their prospective location. A contemporary critic complains that the bringing in of the few families involved great trouble and expense.

The government paid the whole cost of the trip and provided for the maintenance of each settler for one year after reaching the appointed spot. The decrees of the viceroy provided for the welfare of the newcomers as a father would look after his children, going into endless detail. The governor was directed to furnish them with stock and to teach them to look after the same, and the most minute instructions were given as to the plan of the villa, the size of the lots, the position of the houses, etc. It is likely that the settlers themselves knew but little of what was ordered by the decrees. At any rate, they failed to take advan-

tage of some of them.   It was provided that they
and their descendants should all be hidalgos, but
they do not seem to have made much of the honor;
and, further, their settlement was to have the proud
title of "ciudad," or city, but of this also they
were deprived.   It became in the records the
"villa" of San Fernando.

The Canary Islanders were not the only settlers
of the villa.   There were a number of people living around the presidio when they came, and these,
together with some families of Tlascalan Indians,
helped to swell the population of the new town.
Unfortunately they also helped to make a thoroughly incompatible social mixture, and the dis-
cord of their complaint rang to heaven.   The real
"first settlers," who were there already without
cost to the king and by virtue of their own efforts
and expense, could not harmonize with the upstart
hidalgos from the Canaries.

To cap the climax of dissension and disorganization there was a constant triangular quarrel of
villa, presidio, and mission.   The nature of their
differences has already been touched upon.[1]   How
their trifling and childish misconduct annoyed the
intelligent inspectors sent out by the viceroy from
time to time is sufficiently evident from the scoring
they got in the reports.

In the course of time the original friction seems
to have disappeared to a large extent.   The old
and new settlers learned to live more peaceably

[1] See p. 64.

together, and in 1793 one member of the discord-
ant trinity disappeared. The Franciscans at San
Antonio de Valero had been gradually ceasing
their mission work for lack of material, and in the
year mentioned they surrendered the pueblo of
which they had been in charge to the parish of
San Fernando. The four neighboring missions
survived several years longer, either through their
temporary escape from the general secularizing
decree of 1794, or through their continuance in
the condition of parishes; but they had, in fact,
always stood practically apart from the corporate
life of the settlement, on which their fortunes had
little effect. The modern city includes the ground
on which all three of the original elements stood,
and it promises to expand ere long over the ruins
of the nearest of the neighboring missions; but
there seems little reason to fear that the spirit of
commercialism will ever dare to demand for its
own uses the room they occupy.

The name the settlement was to bear remained
long in doubt. That of San Fernando was applied
only to the villa as distinguished from the presidio
and the mission; but as the dwellers in and around
them gradually merged into one community, the
names Bexar[1] and San Antonio struggled with
each other, and the latter finally prevailed.

[1] Or Béjar.

CHAPTER VIII

FIXING A BORDER WITH THE FRENCH

From 1716, when the eastern group of missions was reëstablished by Ramón, till 1762, when France surrendered western Louisiana to Spain, the Spanish and French stood facing each other at the northeast corner of Texas in close proximity. There had been no adjustment of their conflicting claims, and the frontiers on both sides had been pushed forward by actual occupation till they were about to meet. From the mission of Adaes to the French fort previously established among the Natchitoches Indians on Red River was only seven leagues. The situation was a constant menace, which soon came to fulfillment in open hostilities.

After the death of Louis XIV., in 1715, the cordial relations which had existed between France and Spain were interrupted by the regency of the duke of Orleans. This lasted until 1723, when the young Louis XV. assumed the government himself, and the hostility then developed continued for some years thereafter. Orleans, to forestall any effort that might be made by the Bourbon Philip V. of Spain to assert his hereditary claims to the French throne in case of the death of Louis, departed from the traditional policy of his nation and formed an alliance against Philip with England, Holland, and the Emperor. In 1719 a French army invaded Spain, and the outbreak of the war was the signal for like movements in the colonies. In May of that year the French attacked Pensacola, and in June the Spanish soldiers and missionaries of Adaes and San Francisco fled to Béjar, leaving their establishments to be plundered and destroyed by the Indians.

The Spanish documents indicate that the flight was due to an attack made on Adaes by a large confederacy of Indians organized and led by Saint-Denis, but this cannot be true. Indeed, there was probably no attack at all. The ruling authorities in Louisiana did not wish the missionaries to be driven away, and regarded their departure as a most untoward occurrence. Bienville made aggressive utterances now and then, but the Company of the Indies that had succeeded Crozat in the proprietorship of the French colony pursued the policy already adopted of keeping the peace and nursing the intercolonial trade. The policy of the company was Saint-Denis's also, and he could have had no part in any attack on the missions. If they were attacked at all, it was by Commandant Blondel of the post at Natchitoches. He was upbraided by La Harpe for having driven away the missionaries in opposition to the purposes of the company, and was reminded that it was important to have the Spanish settled near the French posts for the sake of trade and of the cattle they furnished; that, moreover, the missionaries could give no offense, and that they had served as curés at the French fort. And Blondel replied that he had gone to Adaes only to save the mission from the Indians, who would not have failed to take advantage of the outbreak of the Franco-Spanish war to destroy it; but the padres, not knowing his intentions, had fled precipitately. Blondel did not add the fact that Bienville had ordered him to attack Adaes, which might not have excused him to the company. La Harpe then dictated to him a letter to the friars, containing a most humble apology. It explained why he had gone to Adaes, and stated that he had taken possession of their sacred vessels to save them from profanation, but that he would restore them when requested. Finally he begged the missionaries to return, promising them all possible help. Whether this letter ever reached its destination does not appear, but it found its way into print.

The occasion brought into prominence a man of the kind that, if they had been sufficiently numerous, might have saved for Spain its hold upon America. This was the Marqués de San Miguel de Aguayo. He offered his person and property for the war against the French and was appointed governor of Nueva Estremadura and Nuevas Filipinas, or Coahuila and Texas. He then raised and equipped a force of five hundred dragoons [1] and two

---

[1] In the old sense of soldiers armed and trained to fight either on horseback or on foot.

companies of cavalry, and in May, 1721, he set out to recover the ground from which the Spanish had fled. How willing the French were to have them come back, he could scarcely have known.

Before this Spain had been forced to bow to the will of her enemies, and in 1720 the war with France had closed. Aguayo went, therefore, with instructions to confine himself to the recovery of the province of Texas and putting it in a defensible state, and not to make war on the French.

The task was easily accomplished. Saint-Denis met Aguayo on the Neches and welcomed him. The Indians gladly received the Spanish, for the business of gift-giving was likely to be more active if the French met with continued competition; and the old missions were soon reëstablished. The distinctive feature of Aguayo's work was the strengthening of the military defenses of the province. In addition to restoring the presidio of Texas, he added another that stood near Adaes over against the French fort at Natchitoches and at the most exposed point of the eastern group. This new fort he called Pilar, and into it he put one hundred men. On his return to the west early in 1722, he changed the location of the Béjar presidio to a more satisfactory spot, and thereafter he established another at La Bahía,[1] on the site of Fort St. Louis, so as to command the only way for ships into Texas then known and used. There he left ninety men.

The French reply was only a little ineffectual

---

[1] Subsequently moved to the San Antonio River.

grumbling and an equally ineffectual attempt to
gain a foothold on the Texas coast at Espíritu
Santo Bay. Bienville protested against the forti-
fication of Adaes, or Pilar, in a letter already mentioned,[1] and argued, with a certain want of either
logic or geographical knowledge, that the flight of
the superior from Adaes in 1719, before the coming
of Blondel, was an acknowledgment that Red River
belonged to the French. Going on, Bienville declared his intention to oppose, in the interests of
his king, this military establishment until he had
express orders to allow it. In a report to the
French minister of the marine, made a few days
later, he explained the state of things on the Texas
border and said, in such a way as to suggest that
he needed inside information as to colonial policy
in Louisiana, that the intention of the Company of
the Indies was to oppose the return of the Spanish,
either to the Adaes, whence he had driven them in
1719, or to the Asinais, and that it had committed
the enterprise to Saint-Denis, who had flattered
himself that he could secure the help of the Indians.
Accordingly, said Bienville, he had issued Saint-
Denis orders, which that official did not see fit to follow, because he thought the interests of the colony
demanded that the Spanish be left among the
Asinais for the sake of their cattle and money; and
Saint-Denis had gone so far as to assure the Spanish commandant that he had nothing to fear from
the Indians. On the other hand, this same double-

[1] Page 47.

dealing Frenchman had told Bienville that he had
the word of honor of the commandant not to establish himself at Adaes.   Bienville concluded by saying that he could do nothing more than to reënforce
the garrison at Natchitoches, which had only fifty
men ; but that he had issued orders to Saint-Denis
to stir up the Indians and get them to refuse the
Spanish anything in the way of provisions and to
intercept the supplies that might come to them from
the Asinais establishment.

Verily the lot of Bienville was hard.   With
Beelzebub directing him at one elbow and Mam-
mon at the other and the imps uncontrollable, he
must often have wished himself either a larger or a
smaller devil in this French *Inferno*.   It is impossible not to sympathize with him.   He played the
hero in Louisiana for the sake of France and his
king, only to see his own high aspirations crushed
by a combination of self-willed and self-seeking
utilitarians ; but history will pass its verdict both
on him and them.

The expedition to Espíritu Santo Bay was made
by La Harpe in 1721.   It was conducted without
energy, and had no substantial results.   The reason assigned for its failure was the unfriendliness
of the Indians.

The Spanish remained at Adaes, and the illicit
trade throve and prospered ; and there was only
one other time when the question of the Franco-
Spanish border excited any special attention.   In
this case the trouble lasted for some years ; and

though the French gave the original occasion, the course of it was confined almost entirely to the Spanish. In its later aspects, it became a personal affair between two officials, which dragged itself out till it became tiresome even to the Spanish chroniclers.

In 1734 Captain Manuel de Sandoval became governor of Texas; and because of the fact that the Apaches in the west were much more troublesome, and apparently more dangerous, than the French on the border, he took up his residence at Béjar, this arrangement being approved by the viceroy. He seems to have been active and efficient in the discharge of his duties; but in some way he incurred the hostility of the captain of the presidio and the settlers of the villa, and they agitated various charges against him. That which they found most effective for their purposes was that he had neglected his duty in allowing French aggressions in the east. This charge was based on a very insignificant fact. Up to the year 1735 the French fort at Natchitoches had been located on what in times of high water was an island; but the adjacent houses, fields, etc., extended westward to Arroyo Hondo and a point called La Gran Montaña, half way to Adaes. In the year named, on account of the overflows to which the locality of the fort was subject and for other reasons, it was moved a gunshot or more westward to a house previously occupied by a Frenchman, where the erection of new fortifications was begun. There was nothing in this to arouse the Spanish; and in view of the fact

that it was practically through French permission
that they were settled in that country at all, their
subsequent conduct appears almost amusing.

Ensign Joseph Gonzalez, the commandant at
Adaes, immediately reported the facts to Sandoval,
who opposed the removal, and a correspondence with
Saint-Denis, then commandant at Natchitoches, began, which lasted through nearly a year. The gist
of it is sufficiently contained in the first letter from
Gonzalez to Saint-Denis, the reply, and a letter from
Saint-Denis to Sandoval. Gonzalez said that he had
informed his superiors of the contemplated removal,
and had been directed to pray the French to keep
within the limits always conceded to France; that
he must demand that they stop the work they had
begun, and that he did demand it, for the first time,
in the name of his king. Saint-Denis did not wait
for three times and out, but announced at once,
with sententious brevity, " for the first, the second,
and the third time," that he was obeying orders
and would continue to obey them. To Sandoval he
wrote, as if with less impatience, that the French
were the first discoverers of Texas; that the French
settlements west of Red River were there at the
time of Aguayo's *entrada*, and that neither the
marquis nor his successors objected to them; that
in 1718 Ramón was furnished with supplies from
Natchitoches; that the Spanish owed their subsequent occupation of Adaes and the founding of their
missions to Saint-Denis himself; that the French
represented the Natchitoches, who possessed lands

on both sides of Red River, without objection from the Adaes, whose claim the Spanish had inherited; that there was no reason why the Spanish should appropriate all the undivided seven leagues between the two forts; and, finally, that he was acting under superior orders and could not desist, that if he were attacked with arms he would defend himself with them, and that the consequences would rest on him that was to blame. This was a dignified and convincing answer. Saint-Denis might not have scored with it on all points before an international tribunal, but it is the best résumé of the controversy that the documents afford. And it seems to have settled the matter so far as the French were concerned. The discussion of it thenceforth is relegated to the Spanish.

Little more needs to be said concerning this episode. In 1736 Sandoval was succeeded as governor by Don Carlos de Franquis, who immediately began an attack on him, using especially the charge as to the removal of the French fort. The attack soon degenerated into a persecution, and before it was over Franquis had to be silenced by a viceregal order. In the course of it, Sandoval was subjected to various outrages; his papers were seized, he was imprisoned and put in the stocks, and a heavy fine was imposed upon him. At length, however, he succeeded in shaking off his relentless foe, and it is to be hoped that he had no more such experiences. The records, at least, disclose none.

For a while during the period of this trouble

there was an unusual strictness on the border. All the intercourse with the French was suspended, and business in that quarter must have become very dull. But this was only temporary. By and by the old illicit commerce was resumed and went on as actively as ever. It could hardly be called smuggling, for that would suggest a degree of concealment that was doubtless wanting. It seems to have become the prevailing occupation on the border, and to have attracted all settlers, including both officials and padres.

As to the matter of limits, it gave no further trouble, except for a momentary protest of the French governor against the establishment of a new Spanish presidio at Orcoquisac on the Trinity, about 1756, and in 1762 it was put entirely out of sight for the time by the surrender of western Louisiana to Spain. But with the Louisiana Purchase there was a resurrection of it, which in its proper place must claim special attention.

CHAPTER IX

THE FAILURE OF THE SPANISH WAY

IT is sad to follow the course of breaking fortune or of social and political decay, or even of that long drawn out existence in which survival is the outcome of a mild environment rather than of fitness. This, however, is a duty that the historian of Spanish colonial enterprise cannot avoid ; and his task is rendered more unpleasant by the fact that much of the energy whose workings he must trace was born of the noblest impulses of humanity. In the "evil dreams" lent by Nature, from which we do not yet seem prepared to wake, the race is to the swift and the battle to the strong ; and if there is one cry that rings from every page of history and biography, it is that weakness and incapacity are punished more than actual misdeed. It will not be so forever, and that it now is serves only to show how far our practice lags behind our ideal of justice.

For more than a century of almost undisturbed possession Spain failed to people Texas, or even to Christianize its Indians. The missions were multiplied, but with all the devotion of their ministry they were ineffective. For the Apache and Comanche of the west they were impossible, and among the gentler and more easily domesticated Indians of the east they could claim little genuine success. Even had the soldiers not done so much to alienate the Indians and paralyze the efforts of the missionaries, the difficulties of the work must have been too great to overcome. The method of confining the natives, accustomed to a free and wandering life, in pueblos in a condition much akin to slavery, and forcing them through a tiresome round of formal services and of manual labor, was hardly calculated to make them love either Christ or the Spaniards. They held together while the gifts were sufficiently abundant, but when these gave out they ran away, and the soldiers were little inclined to take the trouble either to hold or to recapture them.

Almost from the beginning of the work in Texas there seem to have been some among the Spanish who distrusted the system of colonizing by means of missions and presidios, and it was not long until there were very positive and outspoken objections to it. In 1727–8, General Pedro Rivera made a round of inspection among the establishments in Texas. He seems to have found them all in bad condition, and he recommended that the presidio of Texas [1] should be suppressed, and that the number of soldiers in the other three belonging to the province should be reduced nearly one half. In 1729 this was done, and at once there ensued a hot controversy over the matter. The missionaries pro-

[1] Or Dolores, as the documents sometimes call it.

tested vehemently, the governor backed them, and
Rivera replied.   Not being able to secure the restoration of the presidio of Texas, which they claimed
ought to have been strengthened rather than suppressed, the Querétaran friars obtained leave to
move their three missions immediately under its
protection from the east to Béjar.   This change
was made in 1731, but the quarrel went on.   Repeated inspections by military officials resulted,
almost as a matter of course, in reports and recommendations adverse to the friars, and in further
contraction of missionary effort.   So far as this
policy was based on a recognition of the futility of
attempting to civilize the Indians by force, it may
be regarded as wise; but one cannot avoid sympa-
thizing with the missionaries as against the soldiers.
Their views appear sounder, and their allegations
more truthful.   The provocations they had to endure from the vicious presidials and mission guards,
who systematically mistreated the Indians, must
have been enough to destroy all their patience;
and it seems strange, in fact, that they held on as
faithfully as they did.

One of the arguments used against the system
of colonizing by missions and presidios was that
experience had proved the results to be wholly
incommensurate with the cost.   The auditor Altamira, writing in 1744, asserted that the total expense to the royal treasury of the colonizing work
in Texas had been three million *pesos*, and that the
annual cost of keeping up the establishments was

then sixty-three thousand, but that there were fewer
settlers than in 1722. In his opinion the treasury
would never be relieved from the burden — not to
speak of getting a revenue from the province — by
means of the three presidios in Texas. They had
been located with too little regard to the attraction
of settlers. Altamira suggested the plan of using
the money spent on the presidios to pay the expenses,
for eight or ten years at the outset, of colonists who
would undertake to protect themselves. In this
way he thought Texas could be made at length a
revenue-producing province, but his plan does not
seem to have had any consideration.

The courage and persistence of the friars were
not diminished by opposition or ill treatment, and
when the Lipan Apaches asked for a mission in
1745, they were disposed to try it; but the murder
of one of their number by the Indians caused the
postponement of the enterprise for several years.
In 1744 they had got permission to establish three
missions along the river San Xavier, on the western frontier of the traversed region; and by means
of unaccustomed help from a military inspector they
had succeeded in having this frontier strengthened
soon after by the addition of a presidio with a garrison of fifty men. But Indian converts were hard
to gather, the soldiers were unmanageable, and the
work did not prosper. This led the president of
the missions to propose a scheme somewhat like
that of Altamira already mentioned, and which received just as little consideration. Finally, when

the establishment of the San Saba mission was in view and it was proposed to transfer the San Xavier Indians to San Antonio, they all ran away, and the new foundations were abandoned.

The Apache mission project was realized in 1757. The government founded among them on the San Saba River a presidio named San Luis de Amarillas, with a force of one hundred men, and the mission, which was located a league and a half away, was established at the expense of an enthusiastic supporter of the Franciscans, Pedro Romero de Terreros. He had gone so far as to offer to pay all the cost of as many as twenty missions for three years, but the drain on his estate was never required. He did not have to pay the expenses of even one very long. The Apaches (Lipans) were at war with the Comanches, and had accepted the mission for the sake of Spanish help. But, as might have been expected, it was not long before the Comanches came in search of the new establishments. They were said to be two thousand strong; and while they did not attack the presidio, they massacred all the inmates of the mission, except two or three that escaped.

The mission had been an evident failure from the time of its establishment. The Apaches refused to form a pueblo for it, at first excusing themselves under various pretenses, and finally saying openly, that while they wished to be friends with the Spanish, they preferred their wandering life. Still it had been argued that the erection of

the presidio should go on, because its abandonment
might be regarded by the Indians as indicative of
discouragement and cowardice, and cause them to
despise the Spanish arms. So the post had been
held, and the unhappy padres had remained to
meet their fate.

This raid provoked a retaliatory expedition
against the Comanches, which was organized on a
scale rather extensive for the colonizers of Texas.
The force consisted of five hundred Spanish and a
number of Apaches. They marched into the Comanche country, and easily found their enemies;
but these were, according to Spanish reports, six
thousand strong, and they were shut up in a fort
over which waved a French banner.[1] One must
suppose that the Spaniards had lost that fiery courage and appetite for the slaughter of savages which
their chroniclers attribute to the followers of Cortés
and De Soto; for when the Indians sallied forth
to the attack in military order and armed, not with
the usual bow and arrow, but with musket, sabre,
and lance, the invaders fled with great precipitancy.
And shaming still more the traditions of the *con-
quistadores*, they left their baggage and six pieces
of artillery in possession of the Comanches. Such
was the end of the costly and boasted expedition
that was to humble the pride of the Indian foe.

Thenceforth the missionary activity rapidly sub-
sided, and no other colonizing impulse was substituted. The reports and recommendations of the

[1] This must not be taken as proving French complicity.

successive inspectors serve as degree marks to indicate the decline of the colony. In 1767 the
Marqués de Rubí made an official visit of inspection
to the Texas establishments and reported them to
be generally in bad condition. One noteworthy
recommendation he made was that the Apaches be
trusted no longer; that the idea of dealing with
them by means of missions should be given up, and
that they should be forced into subjection by using
if necessary the Comanches against them; and that
those of them who were captured should be carried
not to mission pueblos, but to the interior of
Mexico, and that the tribe should be dissolved.

In the same year, 1767, two new missions that
had been founded for the Apaches on the upper
San Antonio were abandoned, and after the visit
of Rubí both governor and viceroy found it hard
to keep either the missionaries or the settlers in
the province. The changes made as the outcome
of the visit did not render the task less difficult.
In 1772 Pilar and Orcoquisac, the two presidios
of the east, under whose protection the Zacatecan
friars had kept up their missions after the Querétarans had removed their three to Béjar, were suppressed, and that of San Luis at San Saba was
moved into Coahuila. Thereupon the Zacatecans
also had to retreat west. This gave the district
from which the province took its name and in
which its earliest Spanish settlements were located,
the country of the Tejas Indians, back to the natives. The frontier of actual occupation receded

to Béjar and La Bahía; and but for the attachment of some eastern settlers to their accustomed
locality, the Spanish hold on it might have been
completely broken. A few, however, of the refugees longed for their old haunts, and by and by
they went back, led by Antonio Gil y Barbo, and
formed on the Trinity a settlement to which they
gave the name Bucareli. About 1778 they moved
to the neighborhood of the old mission of Guadalupe founded by Ramón in 1716, and there they
built for their protection the Old Stone Fort, whose
recent demolition has been already noted.[1]

Meanwhile the Querétarans had given up their
missions to the Zacatecans and retired from Texas
altogether. Then in 1778 came a new inspector,
General Croix, the general commandant of the
north Mexican States, which had just before been
organized into what were called the Provincias
Internas. He recommended the concentration of
all the establishments at Béjar. The only thing
that would have been left for another inspector to
recommend would have been complete withdrawal
from the province; but for some reason the recommendations of Croix were not considered.

Even the reports of the friars themselves could
not make a good showing for the Texas work.
Padre Morfi, who was along with Inspector Croix
in 1778, said that the establishments at Béjar had
cost the king eighty thousand *pesos* and would not
sell for eighty. The statistics, as well as they can

[1] See p. 61.

yet be put together, indicate that there were two
thousand to twenty-five hundred Indians attached
to the missions in 1762, four hundred and fifty to
five hundred in 1785, and about the same number
in 1793. The character of the *Indios reducidos*
seems meanwhile to have failed more rapidly than
their numbers, and towards the last they were in
the most wretched condition from nearly every
point of view. At length, in 1794, came the order
for the secularization of the missions, and the process began at once, though it was not complete for
some years. The support from the royal treasury
was withdrawn, and the mission lands were distributed among the Indians, who were turned over
to the ministration of the regular, or secular
clergy.

The expiring flicker of missionary energy came
with the founding of Refugio, below La Bahía, towards the coast, in 1791. Twenty years later several of the missions had still a few Indians round
them, but in 1812 they were finally suppressed and
the Indians dispersed by the Spanish government.

One generalization should be made in passing.
With the French on their eastern border the Spanish had practically no trouble. The danger from
that quarter was just enough to stimulate them to
take possession of Texas, in which they were assisted rather than hindered by the French. The
real trouble they had was with the Indians. It was
among those right around Béjar and in the eastern
districts that their mission work succeeded best.

But the San Antonio group of settlements was continually in peril from the Apaches, whom no mission could affect. It was Béjar, and not Adaes, that required strengthening, and soldiers or determined settlers were needed more than priests. There was also great danger from the Comanches, but this was not realized till after the ill-starred attempt to Christianize the Apaches. When Spain lost Texas, along with Mexico, it at least got rid of some serious trouble.

As the declining tendency of the Spanish government in the northern and remoter provinces of Mexico became more manifest, an effort was made to check it by revising the organization. In 1776 these provinces, which were called the Provincias Internas, were put in charge of a general commandant with almost complete palatine authority and directly responsible to the court at Madrid. General Croix, who made the inspection of 1778, was the first to hold the place. In 1785 the authority of the viceroy was again extended over these provinces, and they were divided into an eastern, central, and a western group, each with its own military commandant. In 1787 they were formed into two groups, the eastern and the western. In 1793 they were again consolidated under a government independent of the viceroy, except for two or three provinces that were restored to his jurisdiction. Finally, by an order of 1804, carried out in 1812, the old arrangement of an eastern and a western district was restored.

MAPA

DE LAS

PROVINCIAS INTERNAS

DE

ORIENTE

Map No. 2.   The Eastern Internal Provinces of Mexico, sh

(From a tracing of an original in the Archive

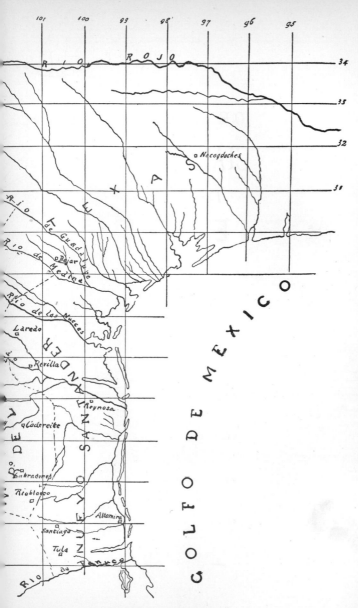

the boundaries of the Spanish Province of Texas.
tillo, officially promulgated in 1816.)

These changes remind one strongly of those made in the Roman Empire as its dissolution approached. They were, however, less rigorous and systematic than those of the Roman emperors. There was a want of complete and definite reorganization with each change extending to all departments of the government. The failure in this respect left some jurisdictions divided while others were not, and the result was the intricate and hopelessly confused system that has already been described.[1]

The weakening of the Spanish hold in Texas was but the prelude to its giving way. With the revolutionary movement that freed the South American republics and Mexico — and Texas along with it, of course — from Spain, there is no reason to speak at length here. In its Mexican aspect, this revolution began with the rising of Hidalgo in 1810. It was caused by various grievances of the Mexicans, one of the most important being the law which gave native Spaniards superior privileges in Mexico to the people of that country themselves, even to those born of Spanish parents. The work begun by Hidalgo was carried on after his death by Morelos, and, when he in turn had been captured and executed, by a number of less prominent leaders, until it was apparently stamped out in 1817. But the revolutionists were only driven into holes and corners and forced to keep quiet for two or three years. Then they became, all at once,

[1] See p. 63.

as bold and active as ever. The signal for this
new outbreak was the news of the Spanish revolution of 1820. This time the movement was successful, and in 1821 Mexico became an independent
nation.

In Texas the operation of this revolutionary activity was to invite filibusters into the province.
The first wave of the revolution had attracted to
that quarter the most important of the filibustering expeditions from the United States, and the
last efforts of the insurrectionists, before the temporary suppression in 1817, had some diversion in
their favor created by another such invasion. This
summary will show sufficiently, for the present, the
connection of Texas with the movement. But the
effects of the separation from Spain were of much
consequence ; it doubtless facilitated the Anglo-
American colonization and simplified the revolution of 1836 materially.

CHAPTER X

MEXICO AT THE WHEEL

THE severance from Spain was a great improvement. It was of incalculable advantage to Mexico itself, which has since attained a development of resources and a degree of civilization that could not possibly have come to it as a Spanish colony. As for Texas, the change enabled it to gather strength more easily for its own self-assertion when the time should come. It had endured the yoke of Spain, with almost passive acquiescence, for nearly a hundred years; but with Mexico it had patience for no more than fifteen. It was, however, a very different Texas with which Mexico had to deal. During these fifteen years the murmur of quarrels among presidial, missionary, and *vecino* and of the appeals for help, which was heard by the viceroy but rarely and by the king almost never, changed to the clamor of those who were accustomed to enforce their rights and in case of necessity to help themselves.

Meanwhile the Mexican leaders, unused to such bad political manners, and not understanding the people whom the ill fortune of Mexico had brought within its boundaries, gave no great heed to Texas, but went on with their petty game of putting down one and setting up another, until it becomes almost impossible to follow. Iturbide, the chief agent in freeing Mexico from Spain, soon threw off his sheep's clothing of liberator and established himself as emperor, but he paid the price of the ambitious for his brief season of authority. After a confused struggle the republicans succeeded in expelling him from Mexico in 1823, and on his return the next year he was captured and shot.

On the expulsion of Iturbide a provisional government was set up which lasted for about a year and a half; but the confusion continued, — in fact it has prevailed nearly the whole time since, until the firm, strong hand of Diaz has suppressed it, — and the hurly-burly of rising and falling heroes of the moment, the storm of vituperation, and the mêlée of actual fighting grew fairly indescribable. Out of it emerged in 1824 a nominal republic, the form of which was patterned mainly after that of the United States; but the essence of it shows clearly the indelible leopard spots of Spain. Its constitution, which became the standard about which the Mexican Liberals afterwards rallied, was fashioned partly on the model of that framed at Philadelphia in 1787, and partly in imitation of the one given to Spain in 1812. It certainly illustrates in a high degree the revolutionary progress towards the establishment of human rights which had been made since 1789, but it serves also to mark the incompleteness of the process. While it destroyed many landmarks of hoary privilege and time-honored abuse, it established the Roman Catholic religion, forbidding the exercise of any other, and it could not go the length of adopting what was then specially reverenced in England and the United States as the great bulwark of individual freedom — trial by jury.

Practically the Mexican Republic was centralized from its origin. Unlike the colonies of Great Britain in America, which had no common superior except in the mother country, the Mexican provinces had been subject from the time of the conquest to a local central authority that was clothed with substantially all the power of the Spanish crown. It had been their ordinary experience to be neglected and left to guard their own interests as best they could ; but this had not begotten in them any desire for local self-government, nor any real conception of manly self-dependence. It was, in fact, between two failures of the Spanish government, the one to take care of them, and the other to teach them to care for themselves, that the prosperity of the colonies fell to the ground.

What genuine republicanism there was in Mexico — and there was no little — was drawn by and by into a struggle against centralism, which the pseudo-republicans and would-be tyrants were seeking to promote for their own purposes. Of this latter class the most conspicuous example was Santa Anna, who after obtaining general support as the champion of popular rights began a movement to overthrow the constitution of 1824 and set himself up as supreme despot. The Texas Revolution was only a whirlpool on the outer edge of the resulting cyclone; but into this whirlpool the " Napoleon of the West " was drawn, and by it he was overwhelmed, just as success was apparently crowning his efforts.

This rapid survey has carried the reader forward over ground that must now be covered more slowly and with more strongly focussed attention.

In accordance with what might have been expected from the really centralized status of Mexico at the outset, the general government, not seeming to think of itself at all as formed by the aggregation of the provinces, provided, in the *acta constitutiva* of 1824,[1] for their erection into states. One of these states was composed of Nuevo León, Coahuila, and Texas. Soon afterwards Nuevo León was made a separate state; but Texas, in spite of all its efforts, remained a dependency of Coahuila until the revolution begun in 1835.

Some of the new states were a little slow in getting on their feet. That of Coahuila and Texas had a congress assembled at Saltillo in August, 1824, but it did not adopt a constitution for itself till 1827. This constitution provided that, while the sovereignty of the state was in the people com-

[1] A provisional constitution promulgated January 21, 1824. The constitution of 1824 was put into effect one provision after another as they were framed, and the instrument was promulgated in its entirety without popular ratification, October 4.

posing it, they were not to exercise that sovereignty except as the constitution provided. Such was the extraordinary principle on which was organized this tribe of Young-Men-Afraid-of-Themselves!

By the constitution of 1827 the state of Coahuila and Texas was divided into three departments: Saltillo, Monclova, and Texas; and afterwards Parras was cut off from Saltillo and made a fourth. The congress of the state was to have twelve members, the apportionment of Texas being two. These congressmen were to be chosen not by popular vote, but by electors. Roman Catholicism was to be the only religion tolerated, children born of slaves were to be free, and the introduction of slaves into the state was to cease within six months from the time the constitution should be published. The governor, who was chosen by popular vote, was to appoint the head official, or political chief, in each department.

The new " Federal Republic " of Mexico moved off on its career under the constitution of 1824 with Guadalupe Victoria and Nicolás Bravo respectively as president and vice-president. Soon afterwards the working of its politics was greatly complicated by invoking the agency of secret societies. For this purpose Free Masonry was used. Immediately after the overthrow of Iturbide the republicans in favor of centralization were enrolled, for the most part, in Scottish rite lodges, which went zealously into politics. As an offset to these was organized about 1825 a new Masonic political party of federal and more purely democratic principles, whose adherents were formed into lodges of the Yorkish rite. These rapidly obtained the upper hand of the *Escoceses*, as the Scottish rite Masons were called, whose leaders began to desert them in large numbers and go over to the *Yorkinos ;* but among those who held on to the *Escoceses* was Santa Anna, as well as Vice-President Bravo. In 1827 the *Escoceses* began to call themselves by the new name of *Novenarios*, because of a plan of gathering recruits for their party by nines which they had adopted ; and late in the same year, in anticipation of a *Yorkino* movement to destroy their order, they issued a manifesto demanding the suppression of secret societies, stricter adherence to the constitution, and the dismissal of the existing ministry and the United States minister Poinsett, who were identified with the *Yorkinos*. An abortive effort followed to support this declaration with arms, and the sequel was the banishment of the leaders of the *Escoceses*, Bravo among them, and the practical ruin of the party.

A new presidential election came on in September, 1828, and Gomez Pedraza was elected president and Anastasio Bustamante vice-president ; but the partisans of Vicente Guerrero, the defeated candidate for president, attempted an uprising under Santa Anna at Perote. It was a weak effort, and Santa Anna with all his force was about to be captured, when an insurrection against the ministry in the city of Mexico drew away the government troops and saved him. The result of this outbreak in the city was the flight of Pedraza, and about a month later Guerrero was elected to succeed Victoria ; and when the term of the latter ended on April 1, 1829, Guerrero was duly installed.

All parties were now too far away from their constitutional moorings for any semblance of orderly government. Under the existing circumstances it was impossible for any one but a man of prudence and decision to rule the country, and Guerrero had neither of these qualities. One success that he enjoyed ought, with wise management, to have given him all the prestige needed for his work. In the summer of 1829 the Spanish sent an expedition to reconquer Mexico, which captured Tampico and set the whole nation in great fear. Guerrero was invested with dictatorial powers, but the Spanish force was defeated by his generals Santa Anna and Terán. The universal rejoicing seemed for the moment to indicate that the troubles of the president were over, but they had only begun.

In the course of this affair Guerrero had taken a step which deserves notice because of its special bearing on Texas. He had been induced by one of his supporters, Tornel, to issue a decree on September 15, 1829, abolishing slavery. Tornel, in a book of his published later, stated that the aim of this was to erect a barrier against further immigration from the United States, the consequences of which the Mexican leaders were then beginning to foresee and to dread very much. The decree had no effect in Mexico south of the Rio Grande, where slavery under the name hardly existed at all; and as to how it affected Texas, the discussion will come more conveniently farther along.

In the decree conferring dictatorial powers on Guerrero at the time of the Spanish invasion, the ambitious and dissembling Bustamante found the means to overthrow his chief and possess himself of the presidency. Assuming the rôle, which is always open to the demagogue, of preserver of the constitution and liberator of the people, in December, 1829, he stirred up an insurrection against Guerrero, who weakly abandoned the capital and left the way open for Bustamante to claim and exercise the presidential authority. February 14, 1831, the unfortunate real president was captured and shot. During the interval Santa Anna and others had held out for him a while, but finally submitted to Bustamante. In Mexican history, however, Guerrero has been placed among the enshrined heroes of the Republic.

For a time it looked as if the country were tired of revolution, and Bustamante would be allowed to govern it in peace, but in 1832 everything was boiling again. In January of that year the troops at Vera Cruz demanded the dismissal of the ministry, and invited Santa Anna to lead them in enforcing the demand. Then followed a bloody campaign between the two sides lasting nearly through the year, and being brought to an end in November by an agreement according to which Pedraza was

to fill out the remnant of his unexpired term.
Through all this series of kaleidoscopic changes it
was somehow remembered that he had once been
elected to serve four years dating from April 1,
1829.

While Bustamante was in power there was
passed another decree affecting the interests of
Texas. It was that of April 6, 1830, which forbade further entry into the frontier states of Mexico of colonists from adjacent foreign countries.
This decree was due to the initiative of Lucas Alamán, secretary of relations.[1] It may be regarded as
the first cause of serious trouble leading towards
the Texas Revolution. It was also under Bustamante, during the troubles of 1832, that Texas was
first drawn into the current of Mexican revolutionary politics.

April 1, 1833, the administration of Pedraza
ended, and he was succeeded by Santa Anna as
president, with Gomez Farías as vice-president.
For the next three years the history of Mexico is
even more confused than in the previous four, and
it is marked by a peculiar mixture of tragedy and
comedy. The comedy consisted in the repeated
vain efforts of Santa Anna to sacrifice Farías on
the altar of reform, while he himself was seeking
his opportunity as the champion of its enemies.
The tragedy lay in his success at last, and in his
driving Mexico through blood and fire unconsciously to her own humiliation.

[1] That is, of interior and exterior, or home and foreign relations.

The new administration opened with loud calls from its supporters for reforms that should subordinate the military and ecclesiastical to the civil authority. Santa Anna stayed away from the capital with the deliberate intention, it was claimed, of avoiding the opposition that such reforms would be likely to provoke, and left the initiation of the work to Farías. In about six weeks, when the agitation was getting warm, he assumed his office ; but a few days later he marched off to put down some revolutionists and left Farías again in charge. Then Santa Anna was captured — doubtless according to a prearranged scheme — by his own troops, who became revolutionists for the moment, and was proclaimed dictator in spite of himself. Thereupon the leaders nearly all ran away from the capital to join him, and a rising occurred in the city ; but Farías got together a handful of militia and put down the disturbance. His force grew rapidly, and Santa Anna saw that the farce had turned into a fiasco. He had to escape and try another plan.

For a few days Santa Anna was in the discharge of his presidential duties again, and then he undertook another campaign against the insurgents, who this time were forced to capitulate. He next played the president a few days more, and then in December, 1833, he retired — for his health's sake, as he claimed — to his estate, where he remained some four months.

In April, 1834, he judged the time was ripe, so

he proceeded to the capital and took final charge
of the government. The reaction against reform
had developed into a strong movement in favor of
religion, privilege, and centralization. It led to a
declaration in May, 1834, by the force stationed at
Cuernavaca, of principles in accord with this movement, and a call for Santa Anna to lead in enforcing them. He accepted the call and ruled as dictator till January, 1835, when he retired again to
his estate, leaving one of his henchmen, General
Barragan, as president *ad interim*. Meanwhile he
had called a congress.

During his active work as dictator, Santa Anna
had dissolved the national congress, as well as those
of the states, and after his retirement the congress
he had called kept up the work of centralization.
In October, 1835, it decreed the abolition of the
federal system and enacted a statute for the provisional organization of a completely centralized
government, the states being turned into departments.

Against this overthrow of the constitution of
1824 Texas alone held out. The two states of
Zacatecas and Coahuila-Texas had resisted the
earlier centralizing measures of the national government; but in April the legislature of Coahuila
and Texas adjourned to escape dissolution by the
soldiers of General Cos, and in May, 1835, the resistance of Zacatecas was crushed by Santa Anna
in a bloody battle. It was only in Texas that con-
tumelious resistance continued, but that far-away

section had to wait a little for its chastisement on the convenience of Santa Anna. By and by he came and saw, but did not conquer. On the Texas stone was broken the would-be arbiter of the destinies of Mexico.

Among the other troubles of Barragan, the president *ad interim*, was an attempt made by General José Antonio Mejía to overthrow the existing régime with the help of a shipload of people whom he had brought from New Orleans to Tampico, most of whom afterwards claimed — though with some evidence to the contrary — that they thought they were simply emigrants bound for Texas. The expedition was a disastrous failure, and it deserves notice here only because it has some significance for the history of Texas, which will appear farther on.

This general, and perhaps in some degrees tedious, survey of the history of Mexico has been given in order to make clear the genesis of the revolution of 1836. The most essential cause of this revolution was doubtless in the conflict between two inharmonious varieties of civilization, independently of any accident of Mexican policy; but the occasion for it — a fact which too many writers on the subject have failed to explain — was a movement that began with the national government of Mexico and spread triumphantly until it reached the northeastern frontier. There it was interrupted by coming upon a sad patch of new cloth in the old garment, a Texas of which neither Frenchman nor Spaniard in the earlier days had ever dreamed.

It now becomes necessary to explain how this new Texas took the place of that with which we have hitherto, except for a few references, been dealing.

CHAPTER XI

ANGLO-AMERICAN INVASIONS

DURING the century in which Spain enjoyed the opportunity to colonize Texas, only to prove its incapacity for the work, had gradually risen the storm that was to sweep the Mexican successors of the Spaniard from that land. But it first gathered, as it were, behind the mountain. Want of Spanish strength and energy at the beginning had suffered the stronger French to intrude themselves between Mexico and the English on the Atlantic coast. This intrusion, however, can be regarded only in the light of an advantage to Spain in its efforts at colonial expansion; for while France strove with one hand to keep back the English, with the other she beckoned the Spanish on to the Sabine.

Time removed the French buffer, and the danger became at once apparent. After 1763 England and Spain were face to face at the great central river; and if France had not been able to keep her old enemies from breaking over the Alleghanies, it was abundantly evident that Spain could not prevent them from crossing the Mississippi. There was another turn or two of the wheel, and the boundary was at the Sabine; and one or two more and it had reached the Rio Grande.

In front of the steadily advancing mass of Anglo-
Americans went the scouts and flying columns.
First were the adventurers who pushed forward
singly or in bands to spy out and perchance in some
measure to enjoy the land, and then followed the
hordes of more steady-going colonists, seeking for
themselves new homes under better economic conditions. This last was just the kind of a movement
that Altamira had wished to promote on the part of
the Spanish in 1744, but he addressed an unappre-
ciative government. It was the certain herald of
a revolution more disastrous to Mexico than the
worst of its selfish politicians would consciously
have risked.

When the Anglo-Americans first entered Texas
the records do not disclose. There is proof of their
presence as scattered settlers, especially in the
eastern part, considerably before the end of the
eighteenth century, but how or when they came
there seems to be nothing to show. The first re-
corded Anglo-American entry is Nolan's expedition,
which took place during the years 1799–1801.

Just why Nolan invaded Texas is not known
with absolute certainty, for the evidence relative to
it is not entirely free from suspicion. He was a
protégé of General James Wilkinson, commander-
in-chief of the United States army, and Wilkinson,
though himself secretly a pensioner of Spain, was
ready to further any enterprise that might be directed against Louisiana or Mexico. These facts
suggest that Nolan may have had his cue from

Wilkinson. It has been surmised that President Jefferson had a hand in the matter. If so, he must have used Wilkinson's agency. The best support for inferences like this lies in the fact that a report on Texas, such as Nolan might have been able to make if he had returned alive, would have been quite useful either to Jefferson or to Wilkinson; and the relations of Wilkinson with Jefferson on the one hand and Nolan on the other were such as might have been easily used to secure it.

There is, however, considerable source material bearing on the purposes of the expedition. According to the story of Ellis Bean, who was a member of the party, Nolan had been carrying on for some years a trade — illicit, of course — with the Spanish in San Antonio, and simply wished to go into that country again; the implication being that it was for trading purposes. The archives of Mexico, as the pertinent documents they contain are summarized by a writer in the " Texas Almanac " for 1868, show the following facts relative to the aims of Nolan : —

In July, 1797, he obtained a passport from the governor of Louisiana to go to Texas for the purpose of buying horses for a Louisiana regiment. He proceeded to San Antonio, from which place he sent a request to General Commandant de Nava at Chihuahua for leave to buy the horses. He got permission and bought about thirteen hundred, which he pastured for a while on Trinity River and then took to Louisiana. But in 1799 a new governor of

Louisiana sent a letter through the hands of the viceroy to de Nava suggesting that foreigners entering the Spanish dominions be arrested, because he had understood that some Americans meant to come in to cultivate relations with the Indians and stir up a revolution. He asked that Nolan should be closely watched. Later in the year 1799 the same governor sent de Nava an official letter recommending that no American be allowed to examine the country, and stating that Nolan was a dangerous man and a sacrilegious hypocrite who had deceived the previous governor to get a passport. He said it was of importance to secure and make way with him finally ; that he was commissioned by Wilkinson to make maps of the country and persuade the friendly Indians to rebel against the Spanish. Accordingly, in August, 1800, de Nava ordered the arrest of Nolan in case he should ever return. In the following October came information from a Spanish official in Louisiana that Nolan was organizing a crowd of thirty or forty men to enter Texas under the pretext of hunting wild horses, and that a protest had been made to the authorities at Natchez, but that they would probably not interfere. In December the same official sent a voluntary statement made to him by a man named Richards who had deserted Nolan on learning his purpose. Richards said that Nolan had explained to him his plan as being to build a fort near the settlements of the Caddo Indians, and from that base to explore the country, hunt for mines, and, after getting horses enough, to go to Islas Negras and Kentucky. There they would be joined by many others, and by that time Nolan would be authorized to conquer Texas.

Putting all the facts together, it appears a probable conclusion that Nolan must have had some such purpose as that attributed to him by Richards in entering Texas. He could not have failed to understand that the number of men he carried would be regarded as too great for any peaceable enterprise, and that it would excite some counter effort of the Spanish authorities. He must have contemplated resistance with arms to these authorities from the outset, but he doubtless relied on help from the Indians to make that resistance effectual.

The expedition set out from Natchez in October, 1800. Just before it started, the United States authorities, on complaint of the Spanish consul, made an investigation; but Nolan's passport prevented any interference with him. Then the consul wrote to the Spanish commandant at Washita to arrest the party, and a Spanish force of fifty actually intercepted the little band of twenty-one, but for some reason did not try to stop it. Nolan and his men passed on; and after losing three of their number by desertion, they penetrated Texas to the Brazos, where they camped and gathered some three hundred wild horses. Then they went to a Comanche village on the south fork of Red River, where they spent a month. After getting back to their camp they were attacked, March 21, 1801, by a force of one hundred men that had been sent from Nacogdoches to find them; and after a fight lasting about three hours, in which Nolan was killed and three men wounded, the little band was captured.

The scene of this conflict was somewhere near the site of the present city of Waco. Those belonging to the party at the time were fourteen Anglo-Americans, one Louisiana creole, seven Spaniards or Mexicans, and two negroes. Only eleven of the Anglo-Americans, besides Nolan, and the creole and one Mexican took part in the fighting. Three of the eleven referred to escaped soon after the capture. All the other persons were tried, and the judge, in January, 1804, ordered their release; but the general commandant of the Internal Provinces objected, and the matter was referred to the king. His reply, made in February, 1807, was that one out of each five — to be chosen by lot — of those who had engaged in the fighting was to be hanged. He was providing for the execution of two, since ten of the class mentioned had been reported to him; but meanwhile one of the ten had died, and the Mexican authorities decided that the execution of one would satisfy the decree. The lot fell on Ephraim Blackburn, who — strangely enough — was a Quaker, but was converted and baptized a Catholic before he died. He was hanged at Chihuahua, November 11, 1807. Spanish justice, whatever might be said of its quality, could scarcely be accused in this instance of undue haste.

The king's decree provided also that the remainder of the prisoners should undergo hard labor for ten years, and they were sent in fulfillment of the sentence to various remote penal settlements. Only one of them appears in subsequent history, that one being Ellis Bean.

No other Anglo-American expedition penetrated Texas for about a dozen years. During this interval the Spanish authorities in Mexico were thrown into a considerable fever of excitement by reports of the coming of Burr. It seems likely that he really meant to come; but whether this was the port towards which his *Buena Esperanza* was directed or not, it suffered a premature shipwreck on the breakers of intrigue and Wilkinsonian treachery. There will be more to say of this expedition in the next chapter, but for the present it may be dismissed.

The next and most formidable of all the Anglo-American invasions was that led by the Mexican refugee, Bernardo Gutierrez, and an ex-lieutenant of the United States army, Augustus Magee. This took on the aspect of a genuine filibustering expedition. At almost every point of contact of United States and Spanish territory there was friction which had been growing for many years, and Kentucky and Tennessee and the whole Southwest were full of men ready and anxious for any desperate undertaking hostile to Spain. Many of them were specially interested in Texas, and they were generally willing to assist Mexico in striking a blow for independence. So when the favorable moment came it was not difficult to find among them volunteers to cross the border and mingle in the quarrels of a people whom they did not understand, and for whom they had little real sympathy.

The opportunity followed the rising of Hidalgo. In 1811 Gutierrez had fled from Mexico with a commission from him as lieutenant-colonel in the insurgent army and envoy to the United States. At Washington he accomplished nothing, and he soon returned southwest as far as Natchitoches, which, now that the boundary had passed to the west side of Louisiana, was again opposite the most salient point of the Spanish frontier. Here he enlisted the coöperation of Magee, who resigned his commission in the United States army in order that he might be free to act. A nucleus for the invading force was organized from the adventurers of the Neutral Ground,[1] who gathered at a convenient rendezvous in their own territory to the number of one hundred and fifty-eight. At the head of this band, Gutierrez crossed the border in August and drove the Spanish troops from Nacogdoches.

The Spanish had due notice of the organization and advance of the invaders, but they were not prepared to resist. The commandant at Nacogdoches reported that he had gone to the Sabine to meet Gutierrez, but had been outflanked and forced to retreat, and that in retiring he had detached at

[1] See p. 130.

the Attoyac, for the purpose of watching the enemy, twenty men, who had been surprised and all captured but one. He said further that, when he gave notice of the approach of the enemy, the citizens showed no disposition to assist in repelling them. On the contrary, they seemed happy, while the troops showed neither spirit nor desire to fight, but became demoralized and fled precipitately to " Spanish Bluff," as the Anglo-Americans called the Spanish fort at the crossing of the Trinity, without even keeping together. The Anglo-Americans followed, and again the Spanish withdrew, abandoning by this retreat the whole of east Texas.

During this time Magee had not been with Gutierrez, but had been busy recruiting and sending forward reënforcements. Before leaving Nacogdoches, the force numbered near five hundred, and at Spanish Bluff it had risen to about eight hundred. At this point an organization was effected. Gutierrez, as the proper representative of the Mexican revolutionists, whom the invaders were to rally and from whom they expected to gather strength for their purposes, was made commander-in-chief, with Magee, who was the real leader, nominally second in rank. Under him were five able subordinates: Major Kemper, and Captains Lockett, Perry, Ross, and Gaines.

In October the filibusters pushed on to La Bahía, which was garrisoned by Salcedo, the governor of Texas, with fifteen hundred men. He marched out with nearly all his force to meet the enemy at the Guadalupe River, but they crossed the river at another point and easily captured La Bahía, securing much booty. There they were besieged by Salcedo for about four months. In the course of the siege he suffered great losses, but accomplished nothing; and early in 1813 he gave it up and allowed the Anglo-Americans and their auxiliaries to move on towards Béjar. But while they were at La Bahía, Magee, who had been directing their operations, died, — one story intimates by his own hand, — and his functions devolved on Kemper. Before the march towards Béjar began, several hundred additional men, partly recruits from Nacogdoches and partly Indian allies, were added to the army.

In March the hostile forces met near San Antonio, in the battle of Rosillo, and the Spanish, whose numbers have been variously estimated at from nine hundred to twenty-five hundred, were beaten with great loss. Two days later the city was surrendered, and every man of the victors had something in the way of spoils.

Then followed one of those horrible events that have been all too common in the wars fought by Indians or by the Spanish. The Anglo-Americans must be relieved of any imputation of complicity, active or passive, in the affair, and thus of all responsibility for it except that which comes of their entering such an alliance. Gutierrez, who had been in nominal command of the invading army but without any real authority till it entered

Béjar, now that he was on his native heath began to take much upon himself. Stating to the army that he thought it safest to send Salcedo and his staff to New Orleans till the war was over, he started them to Matagorda Bay under a guard commanded by one Captain Delgado; but as soon as the party was well out of sight of San Antonio this Mexican brute and his men relieved themselves of the necessity for the tiresome trip by beheading their helpless prisoners, to the number of fourteen, with their dull camp-knives. The Anglo-American officers had Delgado arrested and tried for the murder, but he threw the responsibility on Gutierrez, who was thereupon deposed.[1] The best of these men, who had been brought to Texas by their own reckless love of adventure and willingness to help an enslaved people, now began to understand the possibilities of their enterprise, and refused to follow it any farther. Sick of the business, many of them, including Kemper, Lockett, and Ross, returned to the States, leaving it to be pursued to the end by such of their countrymen as had the stomach for it.

The end soon came. In June the insurgents annihilated one army of more than fifteen hundred men that had been sent against them; but in July, when their numbers had grown to upwards of three thousand, including about eight hundred and fifty

---

[1] Delgado sought to excuse his deed by claiming that it was in reprisal for the unjustifiable and inhuman execution of his father by Salcedo, and that it was done by permission of Gutierrez.

Anglo-Americans, they were disastrously beaten by a force of about two thousand royalists. This, however, was only after a desperate battle of four hours in which the Mexican republicans ran away at the outset, leaving the Anglo-Americans and Indians to fight alone. Only ninety-three of the contingent from the United States got back to Natchitoches.

The subsequent conduct of the royalists, or *gachupines*, as the native Mexicans contemptuously called them, was a fit sequel to the murder of Salcedo and his companions. In winding up the battle they slaughtered the fugitives and the captured. At San Antonio they repeated the Black Hole horror by imprisoning, one August night, three hundred men in a single house, so closely that eighteen of them died from suffocation; and they imprisoned also five hundred women belonging to republican households, whom they forced to cook for them. Finally a body of them swept eastward to Nacogdoches, murdering, plundering, and destroying. After a few days there was little left to show for the feeble colonizing work of a century. The settlement at Spanish Bluff was entirely destroyed. The republicans of Nacogdoches took refuge in Louisiana. How many of them returned, and when, is not yet shown; but the town could hardly have escaped at least temporary depopulation.

The final warlike invasion of Texas by Anglo-Americans was that led by James Long, a merchant of Natchez, who had been an officer in the United States army, and had married a niece of General Wilkinson. The expedition was organized at Natchez, and seems to have been inspired by a feeling of disappointment at the surrender in 1819 by the United States government of its claims to Texas. It was the outcome of a public meeting at which a company of volunteers for the enterprise was raised, the command being first declined by General Adair of Kentucky and then accepted by Long. While the intention of its promoters was to secure, so far as it could be made available, the help of the Mexican republicans in Texas, they perhaps thought less of interfering in the national affairs of Mexico than Magee and his followers had planned, and meant to confine their attention more exclusively to eastern Texas.

After some perfunctory efforts by the authorities to prevent the departure of Long's men, they left Natchez in June, 1819, seventy-five strong. By the time they reached Nacogdoches the force had grown to three hundred. There they organized a provisional government headed by a council, of which Gutierrez was a member, and it declared Texas to be an independent republic. It organized a sort of administrative system, the principal feature of which was an arrangement to dispose of the public lands in such a way as to raise revenue and attract immigrants. It is probable that this feature of their plan lay nearer the heart of it, and throws more light on their motives than any other. When this had been done, five of the leaders were sent out with small detachments to establish themselves at different points along the Trinity and Brazos.

The new republic was but short-lived. Long went to Galveston Island to enlist the coöperation of Lafitte, who had headquarters there at the time; but in this he failed, and while he was gone the Spanish troops broke up his posts and captured or scattered his men. He escaped to Louisiana and, after carrying his family to Natchitoches, went to Bolivar Point, on the Texas coast, where he established the remnant of his men in a fort, pending the renewal of operations. The opportunity for this came with the new revolutionary outbreak of 1821. Long had meanwhile formed a connection with the Mexican Liberal leaders, Trespalacios and Milam, and his next thrust was at the heart of Texas. He penetrated to La Bahía, which he captured on October 4, 1821; but he was soon compelled to surrender with a part of his men. The complexion of their raid as undertaken in support of the risings against Spain gave them favor with the triumphant revolutionists, and they were well treated. Soon afterwards, however, Long was, for some reason never yet made quite clear, shot and killed by a Mexican soldier. After having been detained for some time in the city of Mexico, his men were set at liberty through the good offices of the United States government, exercised through its agent Poinsett.

This was the last of the filibustering invasions.

The main reason for them disappeared when it became possible to enter Texas peaceably. But the province was left in a sad way. To the eastward of San Antonio nearly all signs of civilization that remained after the destructive work of 1813 were now swept away. All the intruders were driven out, and the country was laid waste. Even at San Antonio it became very difficult to obtain supplies. What was left of Nacogdoches by the breaking up of Long's republic was almost swept away by the revolution of 1821. A glimpse of it in that year shows that the Mexican settlers had disappeared — doubtless being simply scattered to less dangerous localities — and the population consisted of only a handful of American squatters, who had perhaps filtered in from the Neutral Ground.[1] An estimate in 1820 puts the whole population of the province, exclusive of Indians, at not more than four thousand. Such was the miserable witness of the craft of Saint-Denis, the patriotic work of Aguayo, the brave and patient self-sacrifice of the missionaries, and the vast expenditure of treasure and blood in the vain effort to plant Spanish civilization in Texas.

[1] See p. 130.

CHAPTER XII

THE FRINGES OF TEXAS DURING THE DECAY OF SPANISH RULE

DURING the first two decades of the nineteenth century, while Spain was making her last desperate efforts to retain her hold in America, and the invaders from beyond the Sabine were engaged in the futile endeavors that have been described to overthrow the Spanish dominion in Texas, the borders of the province on three sides were in a constant state of irritation. To the west were the perennially troublesome Apaches and Comanches; to the northeast were the hardly less annoying adventurers of the Neutral Ground; while along the coast pirates and intruders of various kinds found their way in without opposition, or fixed themselves and remained at will.

Of the Indian depredations of this period there has been written no systematic account. The materials for it will no doubt be found in the Bexar Archives, now in possession of the University of Texas, when they are properly explored; but this will probably be the work of many years. Enough is known, however, to warrant the statement that the Apaches and Comanches were the scourge of the western frontier under both Spanish and Mexican rule. The following statement by the historian Kennedy, resting mainly on the authority of Edward's "History of Texas," will serve as a picture of conditions in that quarter, during the time referred to: —

In the destruction of the Missions, the Comanches were the principal agents. Encouraged by the passive submission of the Mexicans of mixed blood, they carried their insolence so far as to ride into Bexar, and alight in the public square, leaving their horses to be caught and pastured by the obsequious soldiers of the garrison, on pain of chastisement. To raise a contribution, they would enter the town with a drove of Mexican horses, stolen by themselves, and, under pretense of having rescued the *Caballada* from hostile Indians, would exact a reward for their honesty. They openly carried off herds of cattle and horses from the settlements east of the Rio Grande, sparing the lives of the herdsmen, not from motives of humanity, but because they deemed it impolitic to kill those who were so useful in raising horses and mules for the benefit of the Comanches.

The bad condition of the northeastern frontier in the latter years of the Spanish domination was due to a compromise made in fixing a provisional boundary line between Louisiana and Texas. The reader will recall previous disputes over this line. In the investigations in the Spanish courts which took place during the trial of Sandoval in 1738, conclusions were reached which were in harmony with the French claim that the line was properly at Arroyo

Hondo, a tributary of Red River crossing the road from Natchitoches to Adaes slightly east of the middle point. It will be remembered that there was little trouble with the French about this border. In 1762, when western Louisiana passed to Spain, it seemed as if the importance of the limit was forever gone; but the retrocession of that province to France in 1800, and its sale to the United States in 1803, brought the old question to new life.

The exchange of neighbors was in no wise to the advantage of Spain. It is true that under Napoleon France might have proved worse than the United States; for the records show that when he sold Louisiana he had already taken steps to appropriate Texas. But the danger lying in that quarter was never realized. The French claims passed with Louisiana to its new possessors, and Napoleon turned his attention elsewhere.

An American humorist once delivered himself of a bit of wisdom in terms somewhat like this : ' If you wish a mule to stay in a field, put him in the one next to it.' The Anglo-American mule was now in the next field. Taking a large backward view from the present, one feels impressed that it was an unnecessary piece of by-play to dispute over the location of a fence that stood so little in the way, but it was in the usual line of detail in such cases.

The United States, having secured Louisiana, at once set up large claims in Texas. The main object, however, in doing so appears to have been to gain advantage in bargaining for the Floridas, which were then desired much more anxiously than the southwestern territory. In April, 1804, Charles Pinckney, minister to Spain, and Monroe, envoy extraordinary, were instructed to offer the Spanish government a proposition which involved the recognition of the country between the Sabine and the Colorado as a neutral ground. In July the instructions were so modified that the neutral ground was to be located, if possible, between the Colorado and the Rio Grande. The aggressiveness manifested in these propositions and the continued drifting into Texas of intruders from the United States alarmed the Spanish, and led to some display of defensive energy. In addition to a considerable body of colonists that were sent in at the time, a large number of troops were dispatched to Texas. At the beginning of 1806 there were about fifteen hundred soldiers in the province.

The strengthening of the Spanish forces in Texas led the United States to take precautionary measures against their use east of the Sabine. The officer in charge at Natchitoches was instructed to see that they did not cross, and he thereupon asked the commandant at Nacogdoches for assurance that they would not, but was refused. Meanwhile Ensign Gonzales, who seems to have been no more successful as a frontier defender than his namesake of seventy years before, had been sent with twenty men to occupy Adaes and had been expelled by a detachment of sixty sent from Natchitoches.

This insult to Spain and rumors of Burr's contemplated invasion of Mexico drew the Spanish troops to the frontier. In the summer of 1806 some thirteen hundred of them crossed the Sabine and advanced to near Natchitoches. Colonel Cushing, then commanding at that post, demanded their withdrawal; but Herrera, the Spanish general, replied that he was there under orders to defend the territory for the king. Governor Claiborne of Louisiana and General Wilkinson, commander-in-chief of the United States army, went to Natchitoches; the troops there were reënforced; and the demand for the withdrawal of the Spanish was emphatically repeated in a letter from Wilkinson to Governor Cordero of Texas, who was at Nacogdoches, and who referred the letter to General Commandant Salcedo at Chihuahua. Pending an answer, for some reason Herrera fell back to the west side of the Sabine. Wilkinson followed him, and the two armies were soon face to face on opposite banks of the river. But the menace in the situation was not realized. The Burr conspiracy, of whose progress Wilkinson was well informed, was then rapidly approaching its *dénouement*, and the general seems to have concluded that he must go to Natchez to make a parade of thwarting the man with whom he had been in collusion. For this purpose he patched up a hurried agreement relative to the boundary, to which Herrera was induced to agree, no doubt by picturing to him the necessity for checking Burr in the interests of Mexico. Both generals assumed authority in the case which their respective governments under ordinary circumstances would never have conceded; but the stress of the moment was such that their work was allowed to stand, and the miserable condition in which they left the border continued for thirteen years.

The treaty agreed to by Wilkinson and Herrera provided that the neutral ground, which played so important a part in the earlier negotiations of the United States with Spain, and which was proposed first for the eastern half of Texas and then for the western half, including everything to the Rio Grande, should lie between the Sabine and the Arroyo Hondo, the original western limit of the French actual occupation.

Thus shrunken in its extent and moved far to the east from where the United States had last expressed a willingness to locate it, the Neutral Ground became fixed in position and definite in its limits on the east and west, but impossible to define on the north or south. Neither of the nations between whose territories it stood exercised direct jurisdiction over it, and it became the refuge of all sorts of lawless and desperate men. They united themselves in a kind of buccaneer organization and found employment in robbing traders. The authorities on both sides took measures against them; they were tortured and driven off and had their houses burned; but nothing could exterminate them. Finally, however, in the boundary readjustment accompanying the Florida purchase in

1819, the Neutral Ground fell within the limits of Louisiana and disappeared, and with it the band of robbers it had sheltered.

Subsequent to the Gutierrez-Magee expedition, the Gulf coast became hardly less troublesome than the eastern border. It was almost an ideal place for pirates, with its long, bare islands, its river mouths so difficult of access, and its dangerous, low-lying shore. For the filibuster, if he could secure the services of a pilot that knew how to make land safely, it was in some respects a better way in than the Old San Antonio Road from Natchitoches, especially for him whose plans went beyond the revolutionizing of eastern Texas and contemplated beginning with a blow at San Antonio or some still more southerly Mexican stronghold. Naturally enough, therefore, as the Gulf commerce grew and the revolutionary movement in Mexico went on in its fitful and uncertain course, the coast, like the Neutral Ground, attracted a swarm of adventurers.

Of this motley crowd, gathered from all nations, Galveston Island, opposite the bay at the mouth of the Trinity, became the special rendezvous. This locality suited their purpose much better, doubtless, than any in the neighborhood of Espíritu Santo Bay, the old Spanish harbor, which was near the post of La Bahía, with San Antonio not very far away, and thus too much exposed to attack; while Galveston Bay was as good a harbor, and was not in easy striking distance of any Spanish presidio. The occupation of the island began in 1816, when

Louis de Aury, acting in conjunction with the Mexican insurgents, set up an organized government there, with the usual departments, representing the republicans. This establishment was intended to promote the revolution in Mexico, especially by plundering Spanish commerce. Among the crowd attracted thither was Captain Perry, who was among the few that escaped after the defeat of the revolutionists at San Antonio in 1813, and who brought one hundred men. In a short time the force on the island swelled to four hundred — twice as many as the aggregate of Spanish troops in Texas. The principal occupations of this parasitic crowd were — to put it plainly — slave trading and piracy, and it is said that many citizens of the United States sent vessels to share as privateers in the golden harvest.

In November, 1816, came to the island General Javier Mina, a Spaniard who had distinguished himself as a guerrilla chief during the Peninsular War, with a force of more than two hundred men and with magnificent plans for a filibustering expedition into the interior of Mexico. He gained Perry over to his views, and there was a contest for the supremacy in which serious results, and perhaps the overthrow of the new government, were prevented only by the conciliatory policy of Aury. In April, 1817, the whole party, after destroying the "government buildings" on the island, embarked for the invasion; but Aury, who had no heart for the enterprise, after landing Mina and Perry at Soto la Marina in Tamaulipas, sailed away and left them to carry it out alone. It proved a disastrous failure. Perry soon detached himself with fifty men and made his way back to La Bahía in Texas. Drawn away from an attack on the presidio by a superior force of royalists sent to intercept his party, he avoided capture and ended his share in a battle which the failure of his ammunition was turning against him by shooting himself through the head. Mina penetrated far into the interior of Mexico and sustained himself for some time in a brilliant campaign, but was finally captured by the Spanish troops and shot by vice-regal orders.

After leaving Mina at Soto, Aury first stopped for a short time near the old Spanish harbor, Espíritu Santo, and then returned to Galveston Island. But he found it in possession of Lafitte; so he left to share in an attack on the Floridas, taking what remained of his government with him.

Jean Lafitte simply stepped into Aury's place and adopted his methods, but with more selfish purposes of his own. While he may not have been exactly bred to the art of piracy, he had served a long apprenticeship therein, and had now attained the experience and skill of a past master. He had begun his work in the Gulf about 1810 at the island of Barataria on the coast west of the mouth of the Mississippi, where the pirates driven from the West Indies by the English had taken refuge. They are said to have worked in collusion with merchants in New Orleans. Jean Lafitte and his brother had been at first agents in disposing of spoils, which by and by they had taken the lead in gathering. The Baratarians had become so troublesome that the United States government had been forced to break up their establishment in September, 1814. Just before this Lafitte had refused the offer of a captaincy in the British navy, and had then tendered his services to the governor of Louisiana. In December following he and his men had been received into Jackson's army, and immediately afterwards they had played an effective part in the battle of New Orleans. The movements of Lafitte during the next two years have not been traced; but in April, 1817, he had taken advantage of Aury's abandonment of Galveston Island to establish himself there.

There he remained about four years. He claimed that it was only Spanish vessels he attacked; and it is said that he justified himself by the statement that outrages he had once suffered from a Spanish sea captain had led him to declare eternal war on Spain. The story may be true, but his men at least showed a degree of impartiality in their piratical enterprise. It was, in fact, their willingness to make prizes of United States vessels as well as others that hastened their downfall.

Lafitte, like Aury, organized a government with departments having heads, at any rate, even if not a very full corps of clerks. For convenience' sake in preying upon Spanish commerce, they swore allegiance to the then moribund republican government of Mexico, but with no intention of seeking to galvanize it into new life. There was at least a sense in which Lafitte gave strict attention to his own business, and he soon had round him again all that could come of the thousand men who had been dispersed from Barataria, with good substitutes for such of them as were missing. He built fortifications on the site of the present city of Galveston, and a flourishing town known as Campeachy grew round them, much to the detriment of the commerce of the Gulf. But in 1821, after certain attacks on United States ships had drawn the attention of the authorities at Washington to his work, they sent an expedition to the island with orders to break up the pirates' nest. Lafitte made no resistance, but accepted the orders and abandoned the place to a season of rest, after which it was destined for the uses of a new civilization.

One other ephemeral coast enterprise of this period remains to be noticed. It was led by Generals Lallemand and Rigault, who had served in the armies of Napoleon. They had come with a French colony to the United States, and in March, 1817, they received a grant of land in Alabama. The settlement did not prosper there, and they conceived the plan of moving to Texas. In March, 1818, after sending to the Spanish government a rather impudent request for permission, to which no attention was paid, Lallemand sailed from New Orleans to Texas with one hundred and twenty colonists. He established his settlement on Trinity River some twelve miles inland, giving it the restful name of *Champ d' Asile.* Shortly after their arrival the intruders issued a brave pronunciamento, in which they asserted their natural right to the unused land, and their intention to hold it by force if they should be attacked; but as soon as the Spanish came to oust them they retired to Galveston without striking a blow. Possibly they had their revenge on the Spaniard from the decks of Lafitte's vessels, but this is only a conjecture.

CHAPTER XIII

AUSTIN'S COLONY

In modern times men are beginning to understand better than formerly the significance of the function of the pioneer, and to give him a higher degree of credit. The military hero, and especially he that takes the lead in moments of national peril, playing his more dramatic part with the eyes of his countrymen fixed upon him, will never fail of his due meed of glory; but he that plants in the wilderness, "in labours more abundant" and "in deaths oft," the germ of a new civilization, is but rarely remembered as he should be. Others enter into his work and reap where he has sown with little thought of what they owe him for their opportunity, and the contemporaneous historian, voicing the immature judgment of his time, too often gives him but an obscure place in its annals.

This has been in some degree true of the Austins, father and son. It is only of late that the world, with the results before its eyes, has begun to realize what they accomplished. If they themselves, upon the threshold of their undertaking, could have looked forward to the revolution of 1836, annexation, the Mexican war, the acquisitions made by the treaty of Guadalupe Hidalgo, and the marvelous development of Texas and California, they must have been staggered by the consequences that were to flow from their enterprise. Yet this chain of events has followed, "as the night the day," the work planned and begun by Moses Austin and carried out by his son Stephen.

Moses Austin was a native of Durham, Conn. He was trained for the mercantile profession and became a partner in a large Philadelphia importing house. In that city he married Miss Maria Brown of Morris County, N. J. Soon afterwards his firm established a branch in Richmond, Va., and he moved thither. In a few years he moved again, this time to Wythe County, in southwestern Virginia, where he became the manager of some lead mines belonging to his company. It is said that he established at the mines and in Richmond the first manufactory of shot and sheet lead in the United States, and that a brother of his sent out the first sealing vessel that ever visited the northwestern coast of America and went thence to India.

The mines were not productive according to his expectations; and having heard favorable reports from "Upper Louisiana," or specifically the country that is now known as Missouri, he set out in 1796 on a prospecting trip to that section. Traveling over the "Wilderness Road" from Cumberland Gap northwestwardly across Kentucky to Louisville, he next turned west to make his way to Kaskaskia, which was then the most important town on the east side of the upper Mississippi. Vincennes was the only settlement lying on his route. For nearly a week his party was lost in the snow-covered waste between that place and the Mississippi; but finally, just before being driven to the extremity of eating their horses, they reached a small village near the river.

The outcome of this visit to the West was another change of residence. Austin obtained a grant of land, with some lead mines thereon, in what is now Washington County, Missouri. There he built up a pioneer settlement, which, in spite of attacks from the Indians, grew and flourished. When he went into the new country he had to sacrifice a prejudice common to Anglo-Americans in consenting to become a Spanish citizen; but it was not long until, with no change of residence this time, he found himself again settled in the United States. The Louisiana Purchase had extended the western frontier of the North American Republic to the Rockies. But while the change must have been gratifying to him personally, it was one that his colony had no share in effecting. The settlement seems to have "growed," like Topsy, with perhaps as little consciousness of the weight of Spanish authority before the change of government as after. Austin gave attention to his mining business, and prospered to the point of growing rich; but the failure of the Bank of St. Louis, in which he was a large stockholder, swept away his fortune, and he was ready for a new venture.

The opportunity came, as it seemed to him, with the treaty of 1819, which left Texas in the hands of Spain and gave validity to Spanish grants of land that might be made within the limits of that province. He proposed to his son Stephen, then twenty-six years of age, the establishment of a colony in Texas, and after mature deliberation they undertook it. In April, 1819, to facilitate the plan, Stephen went south to establish a farm at Long Prairie on Red River that might serve as a basis for colonizing operations, but for some reason the farm was soon abandoned. Most of the years 1819 and 1820 he spent in Arkansas Territory, of which he was appointed circuit judge. During his stay in the Territory he located a grant of land, on which his brother-in-law, James Bryan, subsequently laid off the town of Little Rock. In the summer of 1820 he met Moses Austin at Little Rock, and it was agreed that the father should go to San Antonio to open the way for the proposed colony, while the son should go to New Orleans to gather immigrants.

Accordingly in the fall of 1820 Moses Austin made on horseback the tiresome journey of more than eight hundred miles from the Missouri settlement to San Antonio, through an almost totally uninhabited wilderness. It seemed at first as if his patience and trouble must go for nought. Governor Martinez of Texas belonged to the class of native Spaniards who were quite unpopular in Mexico, and he was a personal enemy of General

Commandant Arredondo, who he feared would take advantage of any misstep of his to ruin him. This official had given him instructions to keep out all foreigners, and especially Anglo-Americans. He therefore refused to listen to Austin or to go into the question of his having previously been a Spanish citizen, and angrily ordered him to leave the province at once. There was nothing to be done but to obey. Austin was about to start back, but he chanced to meet just then the Baron de Bastrop, a German in the Spanish service, whom he had known before, and who now interposed in his behalf. The order for immediate departure was suspended, the colonization scheme was explained to the governor, and he and the *ayuntamiento* of San Antonio joined in approving the petition of Austin to the authorities of the Eastern Internal Provinces to be allowed to bring into Texas three hundred settlers from the United States.

Before the answer could reach San Antonio, Austin left for home. In crossing Texas to Natchitoches, whence he traveled by water to Missouri, he suffered such hardships that his health was permanently impaired; and in the summer following his return he died, soon after learning that his petition had been granted.

The work left incomplete by Moses Austin now fell to Stephen, who prosecuted it under many difficulties and discouragements, but with tireless energy and unfaltering courage. He was well fitted for it, both by nature and by training. The qualifications and instincts of the pioneer he had inherited from his father; while the large responsibilities previously laid upon him and the share he had already taken in this enterprise constituted excellent special preparation for the duty of pushing it to execution. From 1813, when he had but barely attained the estate of manhood, until 1819, he had been a member of the territorial legislature of Missouri. Then he had gone to Arkansas to assist in making arrangements to plant the Texas colony, and in the interval while the plans were being matured he had, as already stated, served as territorial circuit judge. While his father was busy with the task of getting the grant from the Mexican authorities, he was in New Orleans making arrangements to collect and send on the party of immigrants. There he succeeded in obtaining the coöperation of Joseph Hawkins, a prominent lawyer of the city.

When Austin heard that the petition to establish the colony had been granted and that Spanish commissioners had come to Nacogdoches with the news, he decided to proceed thither himself. In June, 1821, he set out from New Orleans with two or three companions, and at Natchitoches he found Commissioners Erasmo Seguin and Juan Martin Veramendi, with several other Spaniards, waiting for his father, who — as neither he nor the commissioners then knew — had died about ten days before. After remaining a few days in Natchi-

toches, he started to enter Texas with a party of
nearly a dozen men. A report of the death of his
father overtook him just before he reached the
Sabine and caused him to return to Natchitoches
to obtain more certain information; but having
stopped there just long enough to ascertain that the
letters he expected had been forwarded, he followed
on after the party he had left and soon overtook it.
Then he learned that the report was undoubtedly
true. Nevertheless he pushed on with the party
to Nacogdoches and thence to San Antonio, where
he arrived August 12, just in time to witness the
rejoicing occasioned by the news of the independence of Mexico.

Austin carried the news of his father's death at
once to Governor Martinez and told him that he
wished to be recognized as the *empresario* (con-
tractor) himself and to carry out the contract.
Martinez extended to him the desired recognition
and gave him permission to explore the country
along the Colorado and select such a location for
his colony as he might think best. At the request
of the governor, Austin furnished, in writing, a
sketch of his plan, according to which each head
of a family was to have six hundred and forty
acres for himself, besides three hundred and twenty
for his wife, one hundred and sixty for each child,
and eighty for each slave. Single men twenty-one
years of age were to have six hundred and forty
acres each. Martinez gave him authority to promise land to his colonists in this proportion, and to

take charge of the local government of the colony till it should be otherwise provided for. Austin then looked over the country and selected a location for his settlers along the lower course of the Brazos and the Colorado rivers.

He next addressed himself energetically to the task of putting the colony on the ground. On his return to Louisiana he advertised the facts already stated, with the addition that each settler would be required to pay the *empresario* twelve and a half cents per acre for his land. The object of this was to create a fund to be used in paying the expenses of the enterprise, and to some extent in remunerating Austin himself for his services in connection therewith. The plan of levying this contribution was explained to Martinez beforehand, and he stated that he saw nothing improper in it if distinct notice of it were given to every colonist previous to his immigration, but he would not venture an opinion as to how the superior authorities might view the matter.

The first party of settlers was conducted by Austin to the lower Brazos in December, 1821. They went in by the overland route. Before leaving New Orleans he had arranged for the sending of supplies and additional immigrants by a schooner, the Lively, which he was to meet at the mouth of the Colorado. The vessel came, but the landing was made at the mouth of the Brazos. This was possibly because of a mistake as to the identity of the river. The Lively passed on along the coast,

and probably reached the Colorado, but not till
Austin had grown weary of waiting and had left
the appointed rendezvous. The same vessel brought
a second cargo to Texas in 1822 and was wrecked
on the coast. In the fall of that year one shipload
of supplies was landed at the mouth of the Colorado, but it was destroyed by the Karankawa Indians, who added to their mischief the slaughter of
four men. The immigrants brought by the Lively
on her first voyage moved up the Brazos and formed
a settlement, but in the course of the next year
nearly all of them returned to the United States.

The new settlers had many sufferings and dangers to undergo, especially in the first two years.
The failure of supplies and the bad quality of the
game they killed — the mast having failed — put
them to great extremity; and the outrages of the
Indians, whom they were then too weak to punish
or to overawe, made their life almost a burden.

It was particularly unfortunate that Austin had
to leave the colony for more than a year just at
this, the most trying, period of its existence.
When he went to San Antonio in March, 1822, to
report to the governor, he was informed that he
must go to Mexico to get his grant confirmed and
receive instructions concerning the colony. There
was nothing to be done but go, so he left Josiah H.
Bell in charge of the settlement, and set out on his
ride of twelve hundred miles through a country in
which law and order were at that time hardly
known. From Monterey to the city of Mexico he

had but one companion. By good fortune he got
through safely.

It was better fortune still that enabled him, during the most turbulent year of the revolution, when
confusion reigned supreme in Mexico and no man
knew what a day would bring forth, to carry the
business on which he was bent to a satisfactory conclusion. It was then that his fitness for the task
he had undertaken became especially apparent.
When the circumstances required delay he waited
patiently, but when opportunity came he worked
with all his energy. Under the provisional regency
that ruled in the period immediately succeeding independence, his case was referred to the Mexican
congress, and a general colonization law was under
discussion in that body, when it was superseded by a
junta instituyente or legislative committee, selected
from the members of the congress by the emperor
Iturbide. This committee took up the subject and
passed a general colonization law, which was promulgated in January, 1823. Austin had sought to
have his own colony dealt with by special legislation ; but various persons, among them General
Wilkinson and Hayden Edwards, on whom we
shall come again by and by, were then in the city
soliciting grants of the same nature, and for this
reason the congress had insisted on a general law.

Shortly after the passage of the law, Austin
obtained, especially through the favor of the deputy
minister of forcign and internal affairs, Andreas
Quintana, an imperial decree confirming his grant.

He was just on the point of starting back to Texas in March, with his hard-won prize, when another turn of the revolutionary wheel flung Iturbide from his seat, and everything had to be done over again. The matter was again referred to congress, which in April suspended the general law, but passed Austin's case on to the executive triumvirate then at the head of the government, and two or three days later the grant was again confirmed. Thus it will be seen that Austin finally gained his point in obtaining his grant by special act and not by virtue of any general law. But when the grant was shaped by the decree issued just previous to the fall of Iturbide, it had been made to conform to the general law then in force. This law provided that each colonist who was to engage in agriculture should have a *labor*, or somewhat less than two hundred acres, and each who was to follow stock-raising should have a *sitio*, or square league, containing about forty-four hundred acres; while those who meant to do both might have the aggregate allotment of a *sitio* and *labor*. The *empresario* was to have fifteen *sitios* and two *labors* for each two hundred families he should introduce. It is rather amusing to observe that the grant approved in conformity with the law first denies the authority of Austin to offer immigrants the amounts agreed upon with Governor Martinez in 1821, and then proceeds to apportion to each colonist what must have averaged more than twice as much.

A few provisions of the grant to Austin deserve

special attention. The colonists were to furnish
evidence that they were Roman Catholic, — or
should agree to become such, — and that they were
of steady habits. Much has been made by some
of the failure to conform to the spirit of this provision as affecting Austin's integrity ; but it involved no false certificate or misrepresentation on
his part, though the immigrants themselves cared
little for the deceit they practiced. The writer has
been able to find no evidence to support the charge
that Moses Austin represented himself in Mexico
" as the leader of a company of Roman Catholics
who had suffered persecution in the United States,
for their religion's sake." [1] The actual working of
the clause requiring the colonists to be Catholics
can hardly have been misunderstood on either side.
They seem to have compromised the matter by giving up their own Protestant practices for a time,
and by allowing the ministrations of the jolly Irish
priest who went his rounds among them to cele-
brate marriages, christenings, etc. If any one is
to be blamed, a heavy share must fall on the zealous ministers who, after a time, began to organize
Protestant worship in the colony. As to Stephen
Austin himself, what he suffered later in trying to
hold his wayward settlers true to their obligations
to the government from which their privileges were
obtained is a sufficient answer to any charge touch-
ing his own good faith.

[1] Soo Jay's *Review of the Mexican War*, 11; Burgess's *The
Middle Period*, 291.

The final decree confirming the grant gave Austin authority, under direct responsibility to the governor of Texas, and the general commandant of the Eastern Internal Provinces, to organize the colonists into a body of militia commanded by himself, to administer justice, and to preserve good order and tranquillity. Accordingly, on his way back to Texas he laid the subject before the general commandant at Monterey, asking for special instructions. To refer seems at that time to have been the great labor-saving device of the inert and uninventive Mexican officials. The commandant turned the question over to the provincial deputation of the nascent state of Nuevo León, Coahuila, and Texas, then in session at Monterey. The outcome was that the deputation gave Austin the rank of lieutenant-colonel, but left him substantially without instructions, saying that his powers under the decree of the general government were ample.

Austin got back to his colony in August, 1823, and found it almost broken up. Many of the immigrants had returned, and the recruits that should have come in had stopped at Nacogdoches and in the eastern settlements. But he went bravely to work, and the tide soon set in once more. No limits had been assigned for the colony, and the settlers chose their lands, with the old Germanic instinct of robust self-dependence, " as fountain, or plain, or grove attracted them." The result was that they were scattered from the Lavaca to the San Jacinto, and from the Old San Antonio Road to the coast. San Felipe de Austin, on the lower Brazos,[1] became the capital of the settlement and the great centre of Anglo-American interests in Texas until the revolution of 1836.

The failure of the authorities to provide in detail for the government of the colony threw the whole work of organizing and directing it on Austin himself. He took up the burden without shrinking and carried it for five years, when he was relieved of it by the organization of an *ayuntamiento*. During this period he had many difficulties to overcome. The charge of twelve and a half cents per acre for the land, which had been agreed to at the outset, and which was his only means of reimbursement for the heavy expense to which the issuance and registration of the land titles, and the various public enterprises he had to undertake subjected him, raised such complaint among the colonists after a time that the political chief at Béjar imprudently interfered to abolish it, and substitute a fixed schedule of fees for a title amounting to only about one third as much per *sitio*, of which a part was finally given to Austin. Though he was backed to the fullest extent by the Mexican government, his authority was questioned by some of the settlers. The special grants, too, which he was authorized to make, and did make to some, became the basis for charges of discrimination and the

[1] Sometimes referred to in the records as Austin, but not to be confused with the city of that name on the Colorado, which was built for the capital of the Republic.

cause of much discontent. Finally the bad characters whom he had sought to keep out of the colony, and was forced to expel when they entered it, enforcing his decisions against them by corporal punishment when it became necessary, gave him no little trouble. But by the exercise of much patience, tact, and prudence he got through it all with a surprisingly small degree of friction. It cost him, however, a great expenditure of vital energy, the best evidence of which lies in the fact that when the responsibility was lifted from his shoulders, in 1828, his health was, as he put it, "perceptibly declining." It is more than likely that this strain upon him assisted materially in shortening his life, but it was part of the price paid for what is enjoyed by the Texan to-day.

Of course the crossing of the Sabine wrought no change in the character of the Anglo-Americans. They were, like any band of men gathered by their own choice to participate in such an enterprise, the hardiest and most adventurous among the law-abiding element of their kind, being especially difficult to govern by any method which they did not themselves approve. They kept their own institutions, slavery included; and this they did with the greater freedom because the centres of superior governmental authority and power were far away, and the forces emanating therefrom were too weak at such a distance either to lead or to drive the Texas settlers along the Mexican way. Free speech, popular elections, and practical self-government became the rule in Austin's colony from the beginning. The merest tyro in history or political science should have been able to see in the situation the essential elements of a revolution.

It is beyond the scope of this work to follow the history of the colony in detail. After the first two years of its weakness and peril it took deep root and grew and flourished. The work was done, and the result that was to come was thenceforth inevitable. The help lent by other *empresarios* only served to insure its early consummation.

CHAPTER XIV

THE concession to Moses Austin was the signal for numerous applications to the Mexican government for others. It has been noted that when Stephen F. Austin was in Mexico in 1822, trying to secure a confirmation of his grant, several persons were there at the same time seeking permission to undertake enterprises similar to that which he had already put under way. Their efforts were made vain for the time by the suspension, in April, 1823, of the general colonization law that they had succeeded in obtaining from the Iturbide régime. The suspension, however, was to last only until congress could deal with the subject further.

This was done by a new general law passed on the 18th of August, 1824. The previous law had framed a system that was to be administered directly by the imperial government then in existence. For this government the overthrow of Iturbide had substituted what the anti-imperialists intended for a federal republic. It proved, as the account of it already given shows, a sadly abortive affair ; but it was conducted with a degree of respect to federal principles for a time. The new law, therefore, simply laid down certain general provisions, and then relegated the subject to the states for legislation in conformity therewith. These provisions excluded from colonization a border strip ten leagues wide along the coast and twenty along the boundary of any adjacent foreign nation, required preference to be given Mexican citizens in the distribution of land, limited the amount of land that might be held by any one individual, and forbade any tax on immigration for four years from the publication of the law, or any prohibition, before the year 1840, of the entry of colonists, " unless imperious circumstances should require it, with respect to the individuals of a particular nation." This reservation, in view of the prohibition made by the decree of April 6, 1830, is especially significant.

In accordance with the terms of this enactment, the state of Coahuila and Texas passed a colonization law for itself March 24, 1825. The law invited the entry of immigrants and guaranteed them security of person and property and the right to engage in any calling they might choose. They were required to bring certificates from the authorities of the places whence they came that they were Christians and of good character. *Empresarios* were to have five *sitios* and five *labors* of land for each hundred families they should bring in up to eight hundred. The colonists were to be exempt for ten years from all taxes or duties, except in case of hostile invasion. Finally, convicts were to be sent to Texas to work on the roads or in the service of individuals; and at the expiration of their terms they might begin life anew as colonists, sharing in the allotments of land, if they could obtain the certificates of the civil authorities that they had rendered themselves fit for such a privilege.

Now came the opportunity of those who had been waiting so eagerly to enter the rich new field. They began to take advantage of it immediately. Two large grants were made in less than a month after the passage of the law, and within the next seven years dozens of them were secured by men who proposed to bring in many thousand families. Austin himself obtained three additional concessions, and in conjunction with a partner, Samuel M. Williams, still another. During this period, the whole map of Texas was plastered over, from the Sabine to the Nueces, with the claims of the *empresarios*, as if it had been a gold mining region and they prospectors. Ere long it was difficult to find room for another.

This, however, must not be taken as implying that there was a flood of immigration, or that the *empresarios* were accomplishing what they had undertaken. One might suppose, from the energy they showed in rushing after grants, that Texas would soon be swarming with a new population, but it was not so. Texas, even with the boundaries about which there has never been a question, is a wide-reaching territory, and many people are required to make a show on its surface. Most of the contracts came to nothing, and very few of them can be said to have been carried out with any degree of success. The most important of these few were De Witt's, lying to the west of Austin's, in the interior, and having for its principal settlement Gonzales; De León's, to the southwest of Austin's, adjacent to the coast, with Victoria as its capital; Edwards's, the chief town and capital of which was Nacogdoches; Robertson's, lying northwest from Austin's, above the Old San Antonio Road; and McMullen and McGloin's, extending from the ten league coast reserve along the Nueces and Frio towards the northwest. De León's colony was settled by Mexicans; while McMullen and McGloin's was Irish, and its capital was, of course, named San Patricio, or St. Patrick. The effect of the whole movement was to bring in many immigrants besides those who came to Austin's colony, and with the general current floated in large numbers of families, as well as individuals, attached to no particular grant, at any rate until after their entry. The country below the Old San Antonio Road, including that covered by Austin's colony and eastward to the Sabine, filled up with comparative rapidity. In 1827 an estimate probably quite near the truth put the aggregate population of Texas, exclusive of Indians, at ten thousand, while similar estimates for 1830 made the number nearly twenty thousand, or about five times as many as in 1821. Evidently the Anglo-Americans were about to furnish a solution for the problem of peopling Texas with which the Spanish had struggled so long in vain; but it was not a solution in Spanish terms.

One point, to prevent misunderstanding, should have a little further emphasis. The immigration that was procured and directed by Austin himself is not to be regarded, previous to the revolution of 1836, as a stream that was joined successively by others to form a flood in which it was itself merged and lost. It must be remembered that, many as the other *empresarios* were, they brought in relatively few settlers ; and that, up to the revolution, Austin's colony was the predominant element of Anglo-American Texas, and he the foremost figure among the colonists. Nevertheless, the movement had so far widened that it was no longer wholly his own.

It was not long, however, before a few of the Mexican leaders began to wake to the significance of this movement, and to understand the menace that lay therein. During the earlier days of the Mexican republic, in the first glow of triumphant independence and good feeling towards a people who had gone through a like struggle and who sympathized with Mexico in her own, the dangers of inviting Anglo-American colonists to enter Texas were lost sight of. But these pleasant relations were gradually clouded by the working of antipathetic tendencies and divergent interests. Repeated efforts to obtain by purchase either the whole or a part of Texas showed that the United States was not content with the line of 1819, and was not free from a certain itching to secure possession, in some way, of the land which had so

attracted the *empresarios*. This excited the fears
of the Mexican government and, along with other
causes, led it to parallel the liberal policy of the
state of Coahuila and Texas in making many grants
with one of restriction in measuring out the privileges incident thereto. The historian Alamán says
that orders were issued in 1826 and 1827 to refuse
admission to colonists from neighboring nations —
by which was meant the United States — and to
limit *empresarios* to the numbers stated in their
concessions, and in 1828 a law was passed forbidding the colonization of Anglo-Americans near the
eastern boundary line ; but all without effect.

In 1829 Guerrero, who was then exercising dictatorial powers, issued as his own decree an order
abolishing slavery, which had failed to become a
law of congress through the opposition of the
senate. This measure affected Texas alone, since
there were almost no slaves other than peons in
Mexico, and the intention of its main promoter,
Tornel, was to check immigration from the United
States ; but Austin, though he was personally much
opposed to slavery, made such energetic representations concerning the mischievous results that
were to be expected from the decree, that Texas
was exempted from its operation. The colonists
had already begun to take steps to evade the provisions against slavery in the constitution of Coahuila and Texas by making contracts with their
slaves which converted them into peons, but there
was little necessity for such caution. The Mex-

icans were theoretically much in favor of human liberty; practically, however, they cared little whether the Texans had slaves or not. If the Mexican leaders generally were in accord with Tornel in wishing to set up a barrier against the United States, the government was too weak or too timid to execute their measure.

Finally, on April 6, 1830, the Mexican congress, following the initiative of Alamán, secretary of foreign and internal relations, passed a law forbidding further colonization in the border states of Mexico by nations adjacent, or importation of slaves; suspending contracts unfulfilled; and requiring passports from Mexican consular agents for entry along the northern frontier. This law, though it was in general terms, affected only Texas; and from its passage can be traced the growth of discontent in that department leading to the revolution of 1836.

The message of initiative sent to congress by Alamán on which the decree was based is highly interesting to read. While it is marked by a prejudice that leads him to some misstatement of facts, and by little comprehension of the remedies that it would be safe to try for the evils he had to enumerate, it shows that he was much beyond his countrymen in his clear perception of the risk that Mexico was incurring by its carelessness. He speaks bitterly of the insidious aggressions of the Anglo-Americans, saying that they begin by introducing themselves into the country they covet under the pretext of business or colonization, and, when they

have become the dominant part of the population,
proceed to set up unfounded claims and raise disturbances, and finally, either by diplomacy or violence, obtain possession. He says that they have
been using such methods in Texas, — with the collusion of the state government, he charges in effect,
— and that if General Terán had not chanced to
make an official visit to the northern frontier in
1827, and had not observed and reported what was
going on, Mexico would already have lost Texas
without knowing how. The plea of ignorance previous to Terán's report here set up must not be
taken too seriously. If it were true, while it would
not justify any unprovoked interference in Mexican
affairs from without, it would go far towards accounting in itself for the loss of Texas. But there
is abundant evidence that it was not true. The worst
aspect of the case consists in the fact that the Mexican officials were well informed of the mischief
going on in Texas, but did really nothing to prevent
it. Alamán was doubtless right as to the danger of
allowing continued free entry to the Anglo-Americans; how to keep them out, however, was another
question.

CHAPTER XV

THE FREDONIAN WAR

HARD upon the opening of the general *empresario* movement began the trouble with the immigrants which it was sure to bring. This broke out at the spot where conditions were most mature for it, *i. e.* on the eastern frontier at the Nacogdoches settlement. The disturbance amounted to little in itself. Its main significance lies in the fact that it was a danger signal. The Mexican authorities may well have congratulated themselves that it came to nothing worse. But for the conservatism and good faith to Mexico of Austin and his colonists, it would, in all probability, have hurried forward the Texas revolution ten years and annexation twenty. What mighty changes such a happening would have wrought in the history of the United States it is easy to see, but impossible here to discuss.

Probably the reader has already divined why conditions were maturest for such trouble at Nacogdoches. This place was a remote and almost completely isolated centre of Mexican authority. It was the one Spanish settlement surviving on the northeastern frontier, and was completely overrun by intruders. Béjar and La Bahía, the other two

Spanish — or Mexican — settlements, were not reached by the advancing flow of immigration from the east till after the revolution of 1836. At one time Nacogdoches had a population of nearly a thousand, which was for the most part Mexican. It has already been stated that the effect of the Gutierrez-Magee and the Long expeditions, together with the fears awakened by the revolution of 1821, was almost to destroy the settlement. The Mexicans especially fled, leaving their houses and lands to the enjoyment of a handful of more daring Anglo-Americans, most of whom were probably refugees from the old Neutral Ground. Soon they recovered their courage, and gradually they returned to the town ; but it was no easy matter to regain possession of their homes. That they should make the attempt, and that they should have the sympathy of the Mexican authorities of the state, was only to be expected ; on the other hand, one might anticipate that the men who had entered upon the abandoned property, and who had, some of them at least, acquired claims that would in these days be considered good both in law and in equity, would not give up without a struggle. Satisfactory adjudication would have been difficult, even if the parties had been friendly and desirous of coming to terms ; but as they were not, the case was hopeless. It was so much the worse in that, while the state government was with the Mexicans, the Anglo-Americans could count on a degree of sympathy and perhaps of active support from a multitude of their kind who were living along the frontier near at hand. Measuring strength with strength, as the two sides might have been marshaled for the issue at arms, the result was doubtful till the balance was thrown by Austin's colony in favor of the constituted authorities.

One fact that served to aggravate the situation at Nacogdoches was that there was near by a band of Indians — mostly Cherokees recently come from the United States — who were discontented with the Mexican government because of its failure to give them what they doubtless believed they had been promised, a large grant of land in full sovereignty.

Such was the condition of things on the eastern frontier when Hayden Edwards obtained, in April, 1825, a concession for the colonizing of an extensive territory in that quarter, including Nacogdoches. It should be kept in mind that this grant was obtained from the state of Coahuila and Texas, and not, like Austin's, from the national government in Mexico. Nor were the powers given Edwards as extensive as those conferred on Austin. He was to respect the titles of original owners, — meaning, of course, the Mexican refugees, — to keep bad characters out of his colony, to use Spanish in official documents and when the settlements were made to establish schools for the study of the language, and to make suitable provision for the exercise of the Catholic religion. As to his powers, it was provided only that he should raise the militia according to law, and be its head till some other arrangement should be made. Outside of the conditions enumerated in the grant, he was to be governed by the constitution and laws of the nation and the state. When he had introduced as many as one hundred families, the government was to send a commissioner, who should put them in possession of their lands.

This grant gave Edwards no authority to pass on the claims of previous settlers, but he undertook to do so, and was soon deep in trouble. Part of it seems to have been with the settlers to the east of the San Jacinto — and thus within the limits of his grant — who had already secured titles as members of Austin's colony. He also asked of his colonists a certain sum per acre, as Austin had done. The claimants who had been dispossessed by Edwards formed a party of opposition to him, led by James Gaines and his brother-in-law, Samuel Norris, the alcalde of Nacogdoches, and the antagonism increased from day to day. The enemies of Edwards began to send complaints to the political chief at Béjar,[1] and the *empresario* replied in his own defense; but before the matter came to a decisive issue he went away to the United States, leaving his brother, Benjamin W. Edwards, meanwhile in charge of the colony. The complaints concerning the management were continued, and Benjamin Edwards wrote the governor a letter that was intended as a justification; but it seems to have been

[1] The executive of the department of Texas.

taken as disrespectful, and the reply consisted in
the withdrawal of the grant to Edwards. The explanation given by the political chief was that this
was done because of the improper exactions of the
empresario from the colonists.

This was very exasperating; for, besides destroying the hopes that the Edwardses had centred in
this undertaking, it involved great pecuniary loss
and injury to them. Hayden Edwards had acted
very unwisely in assuming powers not conceded in
his contract, and more unwisely still in threatening
those who refused to obey his demands with rigorous treatment which he was not empowered to
inflict; all of which Austin had told him bluntly
in a very frank letter of protest written before the
grant was annulled. On the other hand, the conduct of Gaines and Norris was such as Anglo-
Americans could hardly have been expected to
endure peaceably. The *empresario* would have
found it difficult, under the circumstances affecting
his grant, to avoid trouble, even if he had shown
the utmost prudence; but his want of caution, not
to say his improprieties, lay on him heavy responsibility for the result. By the time the grant was
annulled, the whole affair was so confused that one
grows weary of seeking to locate the blame just
where it should be. Suffice it to say that the Edwards brothers invoked the remedy of revolution.

On December 16, 1826, Benjamin Edwards, at
the head of fifteen men, rode into Nacogdoches
and proclaimed an independent republic, which they

named Fredonia. They took possession of the Old
Stone Fort and organized a so-called government.
The next step was to make an offensive treaty
against Mexico with the Indians, with whom they
agreed to share the territory of Texas. The Indians were to have all north of a line drawn west
to the Rio Grande from Sandy Spring, not far
from Nacogdoches; while the white revolutionists
were to have all lying south of the line. Then the
Fredonians sent letters to the various Anglo-American settlements and tried to incite their inhabitants
to join the insurrection. A number of such letters
were written by Benjamin Edwards to prominent
men in Austin's colony. An appeal to the citizens
of the United States also went to Natchitoches,
but it was sent by a faithless emissary, who gave
an unfavorable report of the affair, and advised
against participation in it.

The rising, however, met with little encouragement. It was only in Edwards's colony that there
appeared just then to be any occasion for it, and
the general mass of Anglo-Americans had little
interest in the quarrels of the local factions at
Nacogdoches. In Austin's colony there had been
up to this time no serious friction with the Mexican
authorities, and the sentiment of gratitude and loyalty towards Mexico in that quarter was strong.
Had Austin been moved less by this feeling than
he was, it would have been easy for him, looking at
the matter from a business standpoint, to see that
the Fredonian outbreak threatened ruin to the

work of the *empresarios*. Farther than this, the
Fredonians were in alliance with the Indians, whom
he and his colonists had good reason to dread. His
mind, therefore, was quickly made up. He took
strong ground against the insurrection, using all
his influence to suppress it, and sending a considerable detachment of militia from his colony with
the Mexican troops who marched to put it down.

First, however, a commission of three prominent
men was sent from Austin's colony to Nacogdoches
to gather such information as could be had concerning the trouble, and to make an effort at conciliation. They conferred with the leaders both of the
white and the Indian insurgents, and urged them
to take advantage of the amnesty which had been
offered by the Mexican authorities ; but the Fredonians replied that they would accept nothing short
of independence, with limits at the Sabine and the
Rio Grande, and that they regarded the Mexican
government as " corrupt, base, and faithless." The
committee reported, in addition to what has been
stated, that the settlers in the neighborhood of Nacogdoches, on the Trinity and Neches rivers and
Aes Bayou, were loyal to the government, though
some of them were playing the hypocrite till help
should arrive.

The stand taken by Austin's colony was fatal to
the embryo republic. Had there been any hope for
it before, none was left after this development, and
its collapse was only a question of time.

The insurrection was not suppressed until there

had been some actual fighting — significant mainly as the first violent clash between the Mexicans and the colonists whose coming they had invited. On January 4, 1827, Norris gathered fifty to seventy men, a few Americans among them, and went to Nacogdoches to capture the Fredonian garrison. It was said that he had expressed an intention of hanging them all, but they had to be beaten first. There had been a considerable number of them, perhaps as many as two hundred, gathered in the town at one time; but most of them had gone to their homes, and when Norris approached there were only eleven whites remaining. These were joined at the moment by nine Indians, and without hesitation they charged fiercely upon Norris and his men, who soon fled. The Fredonians had one man wounded, while of the other party one was killed and several more or less hurt. This was the one " battle " of the " war." Shortly afterwards a force of three hundred Mexicans, accompanied by a contingent from Austin's colony, reached Nacogdoches only to find it abandoned by the insurgents, and the Fredonian republic already dissolved. Austin solicited kind treatment for the prisoners — a few had been captured by the government troops on the march towards the town — and, contrary to Mexican custom, they were released.

The insignificance of the actual results of the Fredonian rising should not lead to underestimation of its potency for mischief. It was ruined by its prematureness, but it was not as entirely quixotic as some have judged it.   The Edwards brothers must have known a good deal about frontier conditions, and they doubtless made deliberate calculations as to their chances of success.   Their mistake lay in resting too heavily on the principle that blood is thicker than water, and in failing to consider sufficiently either the economic influences at work against a general revolution at the time, or the loyalty to Mexico among the colonists, which had not then been destroyed by suspicion and misgovernment on one side and resentment and insubordination on the other.   If the Fredonian republic could have obtained general support among the colonists, or could have stood upon its feet long enough to attract a crowd of adherents like that which filled the Neutral Ground or gathered around Lafitte on Galveston Island, it might never have been suppressed.   Indeed, it probably never would have been.   In such a case, there are three or four different turns that the history of Texas might have taken.   Let him that is fond of such problems work out this one.   If the Persians had won at Marathon the Greek civilization might have been destroyed in the blossom, and if Charles Martel had been beaten at Tours Europe might have become Mohammedan — so it is said ; but neither of these weighty might-have-beens was.   Nor is the world conscious of what it escaped when Fredonia fell still-born from the womb of destiny.

CHAPTER XVI

MEXICAN MISRULE AND COLONIAL INSUBORDINATION

THE Fredonian insurrection failed because the time was not ripe. But it was ripening fast, and the United States government was doing much to hasten the process. While the liberal policy of Mexico was holding Texas open to immigration, and the Anglo-Americans were pouring in under the various *empresarios*, the authorities at Washington were, as already stated, making continuous efforts to push the boundary westward towards the Rio Grande. From 1825 on, the offers made to Mexico, while never received with favor, were repeated most persistently and with most unhappy effect. In 1827, one million dollars was offered for the Rio Grande boundary and half as much for that of the Colorado. Mexico replied by making the adoption of the line of 1819, agreed upon with Spain, the price of any commercial treaty at all, and in 1828 that point was yielded by the United States. Nevertheless the offers continued, and the anxiety manifested to possess Texas bred in the minds of the Mexican leaders intense suspicion of some sinister design, which was easily extended from the United States government to the Anglo-American colonists themselves.

Another ground of suspicion towards the colonists, it is said, was their comparative immunity from Indian attacks. For two or three years after the founding of Austin's colony, in the time of its weakness, it had suffered greatly from the Indians; but as soon as it was felt safe a policy of vigorous reprisal and chastisement was adopted, which quickly put an end to the trouble. At Béjar, however, the depredations of the savages and the insults to the Mexicans were continued as before. This led the authorities in Mexico to suspect the colonists — falsely, of course — of some agreement with the Indians.

If, in addition to the fear of an aggressive design on the part of the United States, and of a secret understanding between the colonists and the Indians, the reader will consider the Fredonian outbreak, with its sudden revelation of the possibilities on the northeastern frontier, he will be in a position to appreciate the feeling of uneasiness relative to Texas that was growing on the Mexican government.

It was out of the suspicion whose origin has been explained that the trouble with the colonists arose. The feeling led to repressive legislation, couched in evasive terms though aimed directly at the Anglo-Americans, which appeared bold and decisive, but which was either receded from on the appearance of opposition, or ineffectively enforced; the inevitable result being to inspire among the Texans first resentment, and then contempt. Moreover the continuous revolutionary state of Mexico itself kept the attention of its people fixed always on national affairs, and made the little share that Texas got exceedingly irregular and fitful. The policy of the colonists was, in accordance with the advice of Austin, to keep as clear as possible of the party strife that was so constant and fierce beyond the Rio Grande ; but whenever the side that happened for the moment to be in power attempted to use stringent methods in dealing with the Texans, it was but natural that they should be identified with the other, and to some extent active in its support. Finally, their resistance to the local administration set up by the victorious Centralists, and more broadly to the whole policy of centralization, drew on them the vengeance of Santa Anna, precipitated the last appeal to arms, and carried the revolution in Texas to a decisive issue.

The first measure of the Mexican government that aroused general opposition among the Anglo-Americans was Guerrero's decree of September 15, 1829, abolishing slavery throughout Mexico. The nature and purposes of this decree have been explained farther back. There were in Texas upwards of a thousand slaves that would have been free if the decree had been carried into execution. From the Texas standpoint, it was an uncalled for and grievously tyrannical measure. To Austin himself, it would perhaps have appeared differently, but for the ruin he felt certain it would bring upon his work. His earnest protest secured from the political chief of the department a suspension of the decree until a rehearing could be had from the president. A representation dwelling on the guarantees under which the colonists were invited to enter Texas was sent by the political chief to the governor of the state to be passed on to President Guerrero. The governor added a plea of his own in transmitting it, in which he emphasized especially the mischievous effect that the decree would have on the prosperity of the colonies. Guerrero received the remonstrances favorably. There was probably but little real interest in the subject on the part either of himself or his advisers, and his administration was already full of troubles; it must, therefore, have been easy for him to conclude that it was better to surrender a point of the Liberal propaganda than to create a serious additional difficulty for his government. In answer to the representations of the political chief and the governor, he issued a declaration, on December 2, 1829, that the department of Texas was excepted from the operation of the decree of September 15. Thus the evil day was postponed for a season.

The next cause of friction was the decree of April 6, 1830. This decree contained provisions, based upon the initiative of Secretary Alamán, for the use of certain revenues to sustain the integrity of the Mexican territory; for the appointment of commissioners to establish colonies of Mexicans and of other nations in the frontier states, and to look after the execution of the laws concerning those colonies; for the sending of convicts to the colonies to work on the fortifications, roads, etc., with the privilege of becoming colonists themselves at the end of their term; and for stopping the entry of foreigners on the northern frontier without passports from Mexican agents, the introduction of slaves, and the settlement of colonists from countries bounding Mexico in the states adjacent to the line of division. It was backed up by a definite scheme for its enforcement. General Terán was sent to Texas for the purpose, with two battalions of regular infantry, a regiment of cavalry, and quite a considerable body of presidials and militia under his command. A dozen or more military posts were established, with garrisons made up largely of the lowest class of soldiery, and the entry of settlers and the issuance of land titles were stopped in all the colonies except Austin's, De León's, and De Witt's. Immigrants just arrived were ordered out of the country, and those on their way in were turned back at the frontier; and some of those who came to Texas at the time have left interesting stories of how they entered by stealing around Nacogdoches, in spite of the decree. It was, in fact, impossible to discover the immigrant who broke in illegally, and it may be questioned whether the law was really effectual; but it did check immigration and irritate the colonists.

The presence of the military reminded the Tex-

ans that the freedom — or perhaps it should be
called the license — they had hitherto enjoyed was
now to be permitted no longer. The soldiers, while
having a wholesome fear of the Anglo-Americans
around them, were sometimes aggressive and inso-
lent; but their insults were never taken by the
colonists in any lamblike spirit. It was especially
unfortunate that John Davis Bradburn, a Ken-
tuckian of most arbitrary and tyrannical disposition, who had gone to Mexico with Mina and
remained in that country, was left by Terán in
command at Anahuac at the head of Galveston
Bay. This post guarded one of the most important waterways into Austin's colony, and it was
important that the collection of duties there should
be attended with the least possible friction. The
matter was of the greater consequence for the
reason that the period of six years in which free
entry of supplies for the colony had been allowed
by Austin's contract had lately expired, and it
was a delicate matter to collect duties from people
who had grown accustomed to having their goods
free. The situation was not improved by an order
closing all Texas ports except Anahuac ; the pro-
tests and threats of the people, however, caused
Brazoria also to be left open.

Terán made things worse by interfering with the
state's administration of colonial affairs. In 1831
the state government sent Francisco Madero and
José María Carbajal, respectively as commissioner
and surveyor, to issue titles to the settlers on the

Trinity. They did so, and in the course of their
official duty established the new town of Liberty on
the river a short distance above Anahuac. Terán
thereupon ordered Bradburn to arrest them for
violating the decree of April 6, 1830. They were
thrown into prison, and Bradburn dissolved the
ayuntamiento of Liberty, established one at Anahuac, and undertook to give lands to the settlers
himself.

In June, 1832, the explosion for which all this
was but the preparation came. By that time the
less conservative element among the colonists became incapable of further self-restraint. Vessels
loaded with goods had begun to pass in and out at
the mouth of the Brazos, with armed men on board
and others on shore in coöperation, without any
pretense of stopping to pay duties. In May, 1832,
Bradburn had put under martial law the ten league
strip along the coast, originally reserved from
colonization but opened later to settlers brought in
by Austin, and shortly afterwards he arrested William B. Travis and some other prominent men of
the colony for alleged insubordinate behavior and
imprisoned them closely. The colonists now rose
and marched in force on Anahuac under the command of Frank W. Johnson. John Austin, — no
relative of Stephen, unless very distant, — who had
brought a contingent from Brazoria, was sent back
home to get some cannon that were there and bring
them by water to Anahuac for use in capturing
Bradburn's fort. But Colonel Ugartechea, who

was in command at Velasco at the mouth of the Brazos, refused to let the schooner bearing the guns pass out unmolested, and it became necessary to attack that post. It was accordingly assaulted, both from the river and by land. There were about one hundred and twenty-five Mexican troops and one hundred and twelve of the colonists. After a desperate defense, in which Ugartechea gave the amplest proof of his own courage, and his men suffered greatly from the accurate rifle-shooting of the Texans, Velasco was taken on June 27.

During the interval, Colonel Piedras, who was in command at Nacogdoches, had gone with a few men to investigate the troubles at Anahuac; but he was intercepted by the Texans and induced to promise that he would have Bradburn removed and Travis and his companions released. This was done, and the trouble in that quarter was over for the time. Soon after, the troops at Anahuac marched away to take part in the campaigns then in progress in Mexico. Bradburn himself escaped in disguise to Louisiana.

In the course of the rising against Bradburn, the colonists had bethought themselves of the desirability of having some excuse to make to the Mexican authorities for this disturbance. It was not difficult to find one so much in line with their own motives and principles as to be a most excellent cover, and to make it puzzling, in fact, to decide whether they were not perfectly sincere in adopting it. Their scheme was to declare in favor of Santa

Anna, who had, in January, 1832, begun a struggle against the tyrannical Bustamante government, and who was then posing as the special champion of the constitution and the laws of Mexico. They had had reason enough to desire the overthrow of Bustamante; and enough, on the face of the matter, to support Santa Anna. So, while they were gathered at Turtle Bayou near Anahuac, in the course of the operations against this place, they defined their attitude in what were known as the Turtle Bayou resolutions. It was a happy thought, and the resolutions soon served them a good purpose.

The reports of the rising that had been carried to Mexico had led to the belief there that the Texans were seeking to transfer their allegiance to the United States. Soon after it was over, Colonel José Antonio Mejía appeared on the coast with a large force for the purpose of stopping the movement. Mejía was of the Santa Anna party, but he had concluded a truce with the leader of the Bustamante troops against whom he was operating, in order that he might avert this danger to their common country. He brought with him Stephen F. Austin, who was returning to Texas from his work as a member of the state legislature, and whose absence at the time of the outbreak probably explains its occurrence. But Mejía was soon convinced of the loyalty of Texas. He was received with great ceremony at Brazoria and immediately presented with the blessed resolutions. Nothing further was needed to prove to him that the conduct of the Texans had been entirely innocent and praiseworthy. But to give him a more complete understanding of their views, a gathering of the *ayuntamientos* of the colony passed a series of resolutions in favor of the party of Santa Anna and insisting upon the preservation of the constitution and the rights of the state. Copies of these resolutions were ordered to be sent to Colonel Mejía and the political chief, that they might be forwarded to Santa Anna and the governor. A similar expression was sought from De Witt's colonists, but they respectfully requested that they be considered as neutral in reference to the quarrels of the national parties.

Mejía spent a short time in the colony doing what missionary work he could for Santa Anna and then returned to Mexico. In a little while the desire of the troops to join in the struggle that was going on beyond the Rio Grande became too strong to resist. At one post after another they declared in favor of Santa Anna and marched away to swell his army in the south. By and by the only garrison left among the Anglo-Americans was that at Nacogdoches under Piedras. This officer was unpopular with the merchants of the town because he sought to monopolize for himself the profits of the trade with New Orleans. There seemed no good reason to the colonists why the man that had incurred their dislike should be allowed to stand alone in opposition to the general movement. They rose against him to the number of about three hundred

and attacked his company. He had three hundred
and fifty men in the Old Stone Fort, but they were
soon forced to leave it and retreat from the town.
Before they had gone far, they declared in favor of
Santa Anna and delivered Piedras to the colonists
a prisoner. They then were allowed to pass on to
Mexico. The last of Terán's cohorts was gone,
and the frontier was once more left to take care of
itself.

That year the name of Santa Anna was much
glorified in Texas, and the colonists sang fulsome
praises of his character and work, which four years
later it must have sickened them to recall.

The disturbances of 1832 and the general unsettled condition of colonial affairs led to the call of a
convention of the people of Texas. The call for it
was issued August 22, 1832, by Horatio Chriesman
and John Austin, respectively first and second alcalde of the municipality of Austin, or the San Felipe district, and the convention met at San Felipe
October 1. There were upwards of fifty delegates
present, and they constituted a general representation of the department, the one notable municipality
unrepresented being Béjar. The subjects specially
named in the call in response to which the body had
assembled were the misrepresentation of the Texans
as seeking independence of Mexico, and the depredations of the Indians; but the enumeration made
by John Austin, in calling the convention to order,
included only the first of these two, and in addition
the eleventh article of the decree of April 6, 1830,

— or the provision forbidding immigration from the United States, — the land matters of the eastern part of Austin's colony, and the tariff. Stephen F. Austin was elected president of the convention, and Frank W. Johnson secretary. All these subjects and several others were taken under consideration, and various petitions to the national and the state government were adopted, among them being one for the free introduction for three years of various articles specially needed in the colonies; another disclaiming in most positive terms any desire for independence of Mexico, but protesting energetically against the eleventh article of the decree of April 6, 1830, and earnestly praying for its repeal; a third asking for a separate state government for Texas; a fourth asking for a grant of land from the state to be put at the disposal of the people of Texas for use in promoting education; and a fifth praying the state to issue land titles to the settlers between the San Jacinto and the Sabine and to establish new *ayuntamientos* in that quarter. The convention provided for the management of the custom-houses, whose functions had ceased when the troops left Texas, until the general government could take charge of them again, but it declined to interfere with the schedule of duties. It adopted an address to the *ayuntamiento* of Nacogdoches requesting that body to look into the claims of the Indians settled near there and assure them that the colonists did not mean to interfere with their lands. It appointed a central committee of safety

and correspondence at San Felipe, which was
charged with the duty of looking after colonial interests in general, promoting closer union among
the colonists, and warning them of the approach of
danger. This committee was given power to call a
convention of the Texas people whenever it thought
necessary, and it had sub-committees in the various
districts of the department. The convention also
elaborated a plan for a general militia organization,
and elected Wily Martin of San Felipe brigadier-
general. Finally, William H. Wharton was chosen
to carry the memorials of the convention to the state
and general governments, and arrangements were
made to raise by private subscription two thousand
dollars to pay his expenses. The central committee
at San Felipe afterwards appointed Rafael Manchola of Goliad a co-delegate.

The meaning of all this is plain. The colonists
intended to discharge their obligations to Mexico
in the most loyal spirit ; but they meant to keep
on the lookout for any encroachment, and to be
ready to resist it to the uttermost.

By the help of information gathered from other
sources the journal of the convention can be in-
structively read between the lines. It shows traces
of the beginning of a factional division in Austin's
colony growing out of opposition to Austin's
policy, organized and led by William H. Wharton,
who had come to the colony from Tennessee in
1826. The general spirit of the policy of Wharton seems to have been in favor of less conciliation

and more self-assertion in dealing with Mexico.
He was a candidate for the presidency of the
convention against Austin, and had the support
of nearly one third of the delegates. Austin appears from this time forward until the revolution
was actually under way to have been more or
less driven by a current of radicalism which he
could not control. It is evident that a majority of
the colonists thought his policy too conservative.
Though his prominence as founder of the colony,
together with their personal respect for and confidence in him, led them to look to him and put
him forward as their leader still, they now and then
broke away from his guidance and adopted measures to which he was opposed. Such a measure
was the presentation of the memorial in favor of
statehood for Texas. But he had sufficient self-
restraint to bow to the will of the majority, even
when it was against his own judgment. It was the
irony of fate that he was sometimes forced to lend
himself as the only effective instrument to the ac-
complishment of that which he personally dis-
approved. He may have been at times too sensible
of colonial obligations to Mexico, but to him belongs
the great honor of giving the revolution clear
moral defensibility.

Neither Wharton nor Manchola went to Mexico.
The convention provoked a storm of disapproval
from the Mexican authorities. The *ayuntamiento*
of Béjar wrote to that of San Felipe expressing
sympathy with the objects of the movement, but

declaring it illegal and ill-timed. The, political chief and the governor wrote official letters condemning it strongly, and Santa Anna advised that General Filisola should be sent to Texas with troops sufficient to take care of Mexican interests. Austin replied to the political chief defending the convention with outspoken frankness. Finally, after a little expenditure of time, paper, and ink, the Mexicans turned again to their old civil strife, and Texas was left to itself once more.

But the revolutionary impulse was gathering strength in Texas, and it could no longer be stopped. All that winter the discussion went on, with the radicals gaining more and more the upper hand, and meanwhile the party of Santa Anna triumphed in the city of Mexico. In December Bustamante was driven from his office, which was filled by Pedraza from then till April 1, 1833. On January 19 Santa Anna was elected president to succeed Pedraza. Now it seemed as if the opportunity of the colonists had come. The central committee at San Felipe called another convention to meet there April 1. Austin and Wharton were again candidates for the presidency of the convention, and the drift of changing opinion appears in the fact that this time Wharton was elected. The convention petitioned for the repeal of the eleventh article of the decree of April 6, 1830, for the modification of the tariff, and certain other things ; but its main work lay in drafting a state constitution for Texas, which was offered for

approval to the national government. This constitution was framed by a committee having for its
chairman Sam Houston, who had just appeared
in Texas for the first time. Stephen F. Austin,
James B. Miller of San Felipe, and Erasmo Seguin
of Béjar were appointed commissioners to present
the proposed constitution to the authorities in
Mexico and urge the petition of the Texans.
Austin alone went. Though the object of the mission was contrary to his judgment, he was the only
man in the colony that had enough influence with
the Mexican government and sufficient knowledge
of the Spanish language and of colonial affairs to be
available for the purpose, and with magnanimous
self-sacrifice he undertook the task. He went to
Mexico, paying his own expenses, and in spite of
the devastation cholera was then working in the
city, labored for six months trying to accomplish
his object; but he was forced to leave in December, 1833, with the matter still unsettled. While
he was in Mexico, however, he had written a letter
seeking to induce the people of Béjar to join the
movement that he expected to see in Texas during
the fall of 1833 for the organization of an efficient
local government. After his departure Acting-
President Farías received information of this fact,
and immediately dispatched after Austin an order
for his arrest. It took place at Saltillo, and the
unfortunate· prisoner was carried back to Mexico
and detained there for a year and a half, a considerable part of the time in close confinement *in-*

comunicado. It is not hard to understand his outburst in the journal he kept during this period: " Philanthropy is but another name for trouble." Finally in the summer of 1835, when it appeared likely that his restraining influence in Texas would be of value to Santa Anna, he was released under an amnesty and allowed to return home.

Meanwhile Santa Anna was concerning himself mainly with the work of centralizing the national government and making himself absolute, but he found time in October, 1834, to hold a meeting of some of his civil and military officials, with Austin present, to consider Texas affairs. After hearing the representations of Austin, he promised that he would repeal the eleventh article of the decree of April 6, 1830, unless mature consideration developed objections to such a course, but he decided that Texas could not be separated from Coahuila, and that four thousand men should be sent to Béjar to protect the coast and frontier.

Disturbances in Coahuila contributed to keep politics from becoming too monotonous in the north during the interval. There was a contest between Monclova and Saltillo for the seat of government which lasted nearly two years, and was terminated in favor of Monclova by the arbitration of Santa Anna in December, 1834 ; but the quarrel was renewed the next year, and, when it was evident that the legislature of the state was about to be expelled by national troops, that body forestalled such action by adjourning *sine die*, April 21, 1835.

Governor Viesca attempted to move the capital to Béjar, but the archives were captured, and the effort failed. Santa Anna now broke up the existing government entirely, and put an appointee of his own in the office of governor.

During the years 1833 and 1834 the legislature had shown itself liberal enough towards the colonists. It had divided Texas into the three departments of Béjar, the Brazos, and Nacogdoches, had provided for the use of English in public communications and records and the organization of a judicial system with trial by jury, and had passed a number of measures greatly desired by the colonists. But in 1835, when Texas seemed to be on the point of breaking away, large bodies of its vacant land were sold by virtue of legislative enactment for almost nothing — conduct sorely displeasing to the general government, as well as to Texas itself.

By this time the excitement in Texas was running high. A war party grew up among the colonists which, in spite of the disposition evinced by the large majority of the Texans to make no hostile demonstration till they were more directly attacked, was difficult to manage or restrain. Some show of violence was to be expected, and ere long it came. In January, 1835, the Mexican authorities had undertaken to resume the collection of duties in Texas, and Captain Antonio Tenorio was sent with a handful of troops to support the collector at Anahuac. He had already had some trouble in discharging the duties of his office, when the news came of Santa

Anna's usurpation in Coahuila. A general meeting of the colonists in the department of the Brazos held at San Felipe to consider the crisis decided in favor of non-interference ; but the war party held another meeting and resolved to assert themselves. A small band of them organized under the lead of William B. Travis, marched to Anahuac, and on June 30 expelled Tenorio and his men, starting them off towards Béjar. The step was generally condemned, but events marched so rapidly that the aggressive aspect of it was soon forgotten.

Rumors of the coming of Mexican troops and of evil designs against Texas now spread everywhere, and the excitement became still more intense. Mexican Liberals like Zavala, taking refuge in Texas from the despotism of Santa Anna, helped to fan the flame. Meetings of the colonists were held all over Anglo-American Texas, and the discussion was fierce. One more act of violence served to cap the climax. After the expulsion of Tenorio, the Mexican schooner Correo, commanded by one Thompson, was sent to Anahuac to look after the collection of duties. Thompson committed various outrages, and finally captured a United States trading vessel on the Texas coast; whereupon a Texas vessel captured the Correo in turn and sent Thompson along with it to New Orleans to be tried for piracy. The issue with Santa Anna had now passed the stage of conciliation, and there was nothing left but for the colonists to organize for self-defense.

CHAPTER XVII

THE STRUGGLE FOR THE CONSTITUTION OF 1824

LIKE the American Revolution, that in Texas was well under way before the colonists were willing to take the decisive step of declaring themselves independent. The revolution passes, therefore, through two main phases : at first it was a struggle for the constitutional principles on which the Mexican Federal Republic had been organized ; and, when this failed because of the complete triumph of Santa Anna in the Mexican states up to the Rio Grande, it became necessarily a struggle for independence.

If the advice of the more radical Texan leaders had been followed, the final issue would have been precipitated at the outset. Henry Smith, political chief of the department of the Brazos, and later head of the war party, urged in a circular issued in October, 1834, that Texas organize a state government for itself at once ; but a reply opposing such a course was issued by the central committee at San Felipe over the signatures of six of its seven members. The seventh was W. B. Travis, whose attitude was consistent throughout. It is impossible for one to read the contemporaneous expressions

of opinion and feeling among the Texans without
being impressed by the patience and forbearance of
the great majority of the colonists. This was due
largely, no doubt, to the influence of Austin himself;
and just at this time the fact that he was a hostage,
as it were, for the good behavior of the colonists
counted for no little in restraining rash measures.

So when Austin returned to Texas in September, 1835, there was general anxiety to know his
views as to the existing situation. The war party
had been thus far, except for the expulsion of Tenorio, — which had been soundly reproved, — and
the capture of the Correo, — which could hardly
be denied approbation, — kept well in check. The
drift of action by various public meetings of the
colonists held during the summer had been, with
few exceptions, peaceful and conciliatory. On the
other hand, a dispatch for Tenorio had fallen into
the hands of the war party a few days before·he
was expelled, and it bore information that the
national troops recently victorious in Zacatecas
would soon be upon the Texans. In addition to
this, orders had been received in Texas in August
to arrest Zavala and the leaders of the war party,
and deliver them to the authorities. No one dared
to try it, but the unwise policy of Mexico was burn-
ing the bridges behind in the march of aggression.
There were calls in various quarters for a general
consultation. The decisive step, however, was taken
and the revolution started with authoritative sanction, so to speak, when Austin gave his judgment

and advice to the people of Texas, at a large meeting held to welcome him at Brazoria on September 8. He expressed himself in plain and positive terms in favor of a general consultation and the maintenance of the constitutional rights of Texas. The consultation had already been proposed for October 15 by the municipality of Columbia, and Austin's speech was all that was needed to secure general and hearty acquiescence.

Of course it was well understood that war was imminent, and the preparation for it went forward energetically. The local committees of safety worked actively, and volunteer companies were organized in all quarters. Fortunately every man had the weapon he needed in his rifle, adapted to hunting and Indian fighting alike, and little further equipment was required.

Before the consultation could meet, the outbreak of hostilities had occurred. The people of Gonzales had a cannon which had been put in their hands four years before to use against the Indians. Colonel Ugartechea, who was commanding at Béjar, demanded that it be given up. The demand was refused, and Ugartechea sent a lieutenant with perhaps one hundred men to take it. This detachment was prevented from crossing the Guadalupe River to enter the town by the removal of the ferryboat, and by misleading statements of the citizens, until a force of Texas volunteers could be assembled. The Mexicans then moved a few miles away, and the Texans marched after and engaged them on October 2 and put them to flight.

The Texans followed up the victory at Gonzales with an energetic campaign against the frontier posts held by the Mexicans. Early during the month of October a band of men less than fifty in number, hastily organized near Matagorda to drive away some Mexicans who were committing outrages at Victoria, surprised and captured Goliad or La Bahía, obtaining possession of a considerable amount of money and arms. About the middle of the month a body of three hundred and fifty volunteers under Stephen F. Austin advanced from Gonzales against Béjar. Meanwhile General Cos had reached that place with reënforcements to the number of five hundred. Early in November a detachment of about forty Texans, sent from Goliad, captured the post of Lipantitlan on the Nueces above San Patricio ; but the prisoners taken were released on promising not to bear arms against Texas, and no attempt was made to hold the place permanently.

The reduction of Béjar cost a campaign of nearly two months. October 28 a detachment of about one hundred men under Colonel James Bowie and Captain J. W. Fannin defeated a much larger force of Mexicans near Mission Concepción. A council of war was then held to consider the question of storming Béjar ; but owing to the strength of the fortifications and the want of artillery to breach them, it was decided not to make the attempt. On November 25 Austin, who had been appointed by the consultation, then in session at San Felipe, jointly with Branch T. Archer and William H. Wharton, to go on a mission to the United States, turned over his command to Colonel Edward Burleson and left to undertake his new duties. Previous to this the Texan army had received considerable reënforcements, among them being two companies from New Orleans and one from Mississippi, but there was much disorganization in the ranks, and men were leaving constantly. The vain siege was continued until December 4, when it appeared to be about to end in disorder; but Benjamin R. Milam, acting by Burleson's authority and taking advantage of a moment of enthusiasm among the men, made a sudden ringing call for volunteers to follow him in an assault on the city, and the hesitation was at an end. On the morning of the 5th the Texans began fighting their way in from house to house with the most desperate courage and determination. On the 9th the fighting was stopped by negotiations for a surrender, and on the 11th the capitulation was signed. Cos and his officers gave their parole not to resist further the struggle for the constitution of 1824. He was to take a guard of regular infantry and cavalry and convoy the convict soldiers, of which his army was largely composed, beyond the Rio Grande. The men, except the convicts, were left in possession of their arms and effects with permission to remain or to go whither they chose. On December 14 Cos marched away with a few more than eleven hundred men, leaving some two hundred who preferred to stay. The losses in this affair were for the Texans two killed — Milam being one of them — and twenty-six wounded, and for the Mexicans altogether probably one hundred and fifty.

The capture of Cos at Béjar had left not a man in arms against the Texans north of the Rio Grande. If the Anglo-Americans were sincere in the declaration that their purpose was simply to restore the constitution of 1824 and in the promise which we shall see a little further on they had made to coöperate with the Mexican Liberals, the next step would naturally be to carry the war into the interior of Mexico and undertake the overthrow of the Centralists throughout the republic. In conformity with this idea of the object of the revolution and proper management of the campaign, an expedition against Matamoras was planned. But at this point differences which had already begun to show themselves among the Texans in council and in the field began to work with such mischievous influence and strength that operations both offensive and defensive were almost paralyzed. The truth is that the disasters which marked the campaign of 1836 up to the very moment of the victory at San Jacinto were only the legitimate result of the cross-purposes and counter-efforts in Texas during the previous fall and winter.

While the siege of Béjar was in progress, the consultation gathered for the appointed meeting. Owing to the absence of many delegates who were with the army, there was no quorum. The members present were also anxious to take part in the fighting ; so, after a temporary organization on October 16, the body adjourned till the next day, and then till November 1. It was not able to effect a permanent organization till November 3, and it remained in session twelve days. In his speech before proceeding to business the president, Branch T. Archer, declared that he did not view the struggle in which they were engaged as that of " Texas battling alone for her rights and liberties," but that he felt they had undertaken " the work of laying the cornerstone of liberty in the great Mexican Republic." A committee of twelve, one from each municipality, — i. e. each locally organized district, — was appointed to draw up a declaration defining the attitude of the Texans. The chairman of this committee was J. A. Wharton of Columbia, brother of W. H. Wharton, who was with the army at Béjar. On the 4th Wharton reported for the committee ; but the declaration, which has not been preserved,[1] must have been too radical to suit the majority, for a debate followed as to whether it should be in favor of independence for Texas, or of the principles of the constitution of 1824. Sam Houston, who seems to have left Texas soon after the convention of 1833 and to have returned just previous to the consultation, and who was a delegate from Nacogdoches, offered a resolution instructing

[1] Since this statement was written, a document which may be the declaration has been discovered among the archives in the state capitol, but it has not yet been positively identified.

the committee to declare in favor of the constitution
of 1824, but the opposition of Wharton caused him
to withdraw it.   On the 6th the decisive question
was put, and fifteen votes were in favor of declaring
absolute independence, while thirty-three favored
declaring for the constitution of 1824.   The opposition of Wharton prevented the entry of the ayes
and noes in the journal, but the votes of the most
prominent members can be determined with a fair
degree of certainty.

The report of Wharton's committee was reformed
to agree with the will of the majority, and on the
7th the declaration was adopted.   It asserted that
the Texans had taken up arms " in defense of the
republican principles of the federal constitution of
Mexico, of eighteen and twenty-four ; " that they
were " no longer morally or civilly bound by the
compact of union," but that out of generosity and
sympathy they offered help to those Mexican states
that would make a stand against military despotism ;
that they claimed the right to govern themselves
independently or as they might think best while the
disorganization of the federal government continued, but that they would remain faithful to Mexico
while it was governed by the constitution of 1824 ;
and that they would receive as citizens and reward
with land all who came to their help in this struggle.   The word " republican " was inserted before
" principles " in the first section by amendment
just on the eve of adoption.   This declaration,
made consciously and after mature deliberation,

was conciliatory beyond what could have been reasonably expected; and the failure of Mexico to meet it with any sort of concession, though none was to be looked for except through the overthrow of Santa Anna, justifies the revolution fully. It was likewise the extreme and menacing persistence of the Mexican Centralists and the inability of prostrate Liberalism to rise again at the call of its champion that drove Texas from this halfway house of the constitution of 1824 to the final lodge of independence. That the declaration was perhaps dictated in considerable measure by expediency does not alter the case. It was at least no repetition of the Turtle Bayou resolutions. The time for temporizing or extenuating was past, and the policy avowed by the Texans was that which they were at the moment resolved to pursue.

Having thus defined the object of the Texans in taking up arms, the consultation proceeded to organize a provisional government. The scheme adopted was double, one part providing for a civil and the other for a military organization; and both of them were triumphs of potential confusion and conflict of authority. The civil government was to consist of a governor and lieutenant-governor elected by the consultation, and a council made up of one member from each municipality elected by its delegates. The governor and council had ill-defined and practically coördinate powers, those of the council being mainly legislative but partly appointive and advisory, and there was no provi-

sion against deadlocks. It would have been difficult to frame an instrument less adapted to the
emergency. The plan for the military organization was, if possible, even worse. It provided for
a regular army of eleven hundred and twenty men
to serve for two years, or for the war, and a militia
made up of all able-bodied men in Texas. The
regulars were to be headed by a major-general,
who was to be commander-in-chief of all the forces
called into public service during the war. He was
to be appointed by the consultation, commissioned
by the governor, and subject to the orders of the
governor and council. In the field the regular
army was to be subject to the rules, regulations,
and discipline of that of the United States, so far
as applicable to Texas conditions. But on the day
before its adjournment the consultation took action
by which it expressly denied the provisional government any control over the volunteer army before Béjar.

In the election of officers for the provisional
government, Henry Smith, who had been one of
the most radical, first of the war party and later
of the independence party, was elected governor,
receiving thirty-one votes, as against twenty-two
cast for Stephen F. Austin. James W. Robinson
was elected lieutenant-governor, and Sam Houston
major-general of the armies of Texas; and Branch
T. Archer, William H. Wharton, and Stephen F.
Austin were appointed commissioners to the United
States.

Having completed the organization of the provisional government and commended to it the proposed expedition against Matamoras, the consultation adjourned to meet March 1, 1836, unless sooner called together by the governor and council.

It was but a short time till friction was developed between the governor and council, which grew at length into a violent and unseemly quarrel. The first steps towards it bore a rather ridiculous aspect. The plan of the provisional government as adopted by the consultation did not confer on the governor the veto power; but the council in passing an ordinance to govern the methods of legislation made provision for the exercise of this power and thus assumed that he was to have it. The governor vetoed this ordinance itself, but thenceforth exercised the power it seemed to concede, and there was no protest except where his negative was invoked against the appointments of the council. Vetoes soon came thick and fast, and the council might have had reason to repent its concession but for the little difficulty there was in securing a two thirds majority to override them. The fundamental difference between the governor and council was that it was in favor of carrying out the policy adopted by the consultation in its pronunciamento of November 7, and thus coöperating with the Mexican Liberals in restoring the constitution of 1824; while he wished absolute independence and was opposed to any dealing with the Mexicans. But opposition extended to many

matters of detail, such as the method of drawing
on the treasury, the appointment of certain officials, and the question of allowing Mexican Liberals
resident in Texas to vote for members of the convention that it was desired to call.

The most serious difference, however, was concerning the Matamoras expedition. After the fall
of Béjar there was a general feeling that such an
enterprise would be feasible and expedient. About
the middle of December Smith himself was so far
influenced by this feeling that he ordered General
Sam Houston to appoint Colonel Bowie to lead the
expedition, and the appointment was made; but
for some reason Bowie did not go. A few days
later the governor received a letter from Frank W.
Johnson, who had succeeded Burleson in command
of the volunteer army, asking, because of the
threatening aspect of affairs beyond the Rio
Grande, for help to strengthen the frontier outposts. The letter was referred to the council, and
in a report thereon made December 25 the committee on military affairs, after presenting various
considerations in favor of immediate active operations against Matamoras, recommended the concentration of the troops on the frontier. The council
laid the report on the table for the time; but
Houston wrote the governor, in relation to it, protesting against being ordered away from his central
position at San Felipe to an outpost, where he said
a subordinate could "discharge every duty." On
January 3 Johnson, who had come to San Felipe

for the purpose, reported that he had already
ordered the expedition under authority of an official letter directed to his predecessor in the command of the volunteers, General Burleson, and
that the troops had chosen him to lead it. He
asked the council to ratify the plan, and it did so
promptly, taking steps to provide for coöperation
by sea. On the 6th, however, for reasons given in
a letter not preserved, he withdrew from the affair;
but on the 7th he changed his mind again and
informed the council that he would go. Meanwhile Fannin had been authorized to lead the expedition. The council now restored Johnson's
authority, without taking away Fannin's. On the
8th Fannin published a call for volunteers, who
were to rendezvous at San Patricio between the
24th and the 27th. On the 10th Johnson issued
a proclamation, also calling for volunteers, and
stating that the " whole of the volunteer army of
Texas " was expected to advance from San Patricio between the 25th and the 30th. Houston com-
plained that he was being superseded, and Governor Smith, who was in sympathy with him, saw
that something must now be done by the major-
general himself. So the governor gave him orders
to go to the frontier.

The quarrel between the governor and council
now reached its culmination. This was brought
on by a report that was made to Houston by Lieutenant-Colonel Neill, in command at Béjar, and
forwarded to the governor, in a letter dated Jan-

uary 6. It stated that the volunteers on leaving
for Matamoras had taken all available supplies
and left the men at the post destitute of actual
necessities. Smith was utterly beside himself, and
on January 10, with the fever of his rage hot
within him, he penned an intemperate message to
the council, calling some of its members whom he
did not name " Judases," " scoundrels," and " par-
ricides," and using expressions towards them that
were still more offensive. He concluded by informing them that the body was adjourned until
March 1, unless it should be convened by proclamation at an earlier date, and that he would continue to do his duty as commander-in-chief of the
army and navy and as chief executive.

The council made a severe and dignified reply,
in which it characterized the message as " unwor-
thy of, and disgraceful to the office whence it em-
anated, and as an outrageous libel on the body to
whom it is addressed." It followed this up with
a series of resolutions ordering the governor " to
cease the functions of his office and to be held to
answer to the General Council " on an impeachment to be preferred against him by that body,
and recognizing Lieutenant-Governor Robinson as
acting governor. An exculpatory address was
issued to the people of Texas by the council, and
charges and specifications against the governor
were made out and he was furnished with a copy.
He was informed that he might, if he preferred,
answer to the convention that was to meet in

March. On the 12th Smith sent the council another message which, though rather offensive in its demands, was intended to be conciliatory; but the council replied that the time for compromise and conciliation was past. On the 13th he sent a communication stating, among other things, that he held himself ready to answer his impeachment before the convention. On the same day the council passed a resolution directing the secretary of the governor, Charles B. Stewart, who was also recording clerk of the council, to communicate officially with Robinson instead of Smith, and to hold the archives of the executive office subject to the order of Robinson. On the 14th it adopted a resolution requesting Governor Smith to deliver to its president the public correspondence and documents then in his hands or to be received by him. On the 16th Stewart was suspended from office and fined twenty-five hundred dollars for contempt of the council in not obeying the resolution of the 13th. On February 3 Smith sent the council a demand for certain "executive papers," threatening in case of non-compliance to order the arrest of the members and their transmission to Béjar to be tried by martial law. When the convention met, both sides presented statements concerning the quarrel; but that body replied simply by asking for the documents in possession of both, and refused to go farther into the affair. Thus ended an episode as ridiculous as it was disgraceful.

But it was also supremely mischievous; for it

ruined the campaign so well begun by the capture
of Béjar and almost paralyzed the defense of Texas.
The Matamoras expedition was broken up, but the
isolated frontier outposts were neither abandoned,
nor were they adequately defended. What the
result of a little more energy directed that way
would have been remains among the untried issues.
There are some who believe that it would have been
effective only in dividing and weakening the Texan
forces; but others are of the opinion that if the
invading Mexicans had been met on the frontier
line with the whole strength of Texas, and with
the spirit afterwards displayed at the Alamo, they
would never have reached the Anglo-American settlements at all. However that may be, with Smith
and Houston pulling one way and the council, to
gether with Johnson, Fannin, and a crowd of minor
leaders, the other, the outcome was at least temporarily disastrous.

In response to appeals for reënforcements from
Lieutenant-Colonel Neill in command of the Alamo,
General Houston dispatched Colonel Bowie with a
small force, instructing Neill to demolish the fortifications at Béjar and carry off the artillery. Neill,
however, was without teams to bring away the guns,
so he did not obey the order. Governor Smith sent
Travis also, with the men in his detachment. Soon
afterwards Neill left for home, because of ill health,
leaving Travis at the head of the troops. The latter
claimed command of the regulars and the volunteer
cavalry, while Bowie was at the head of the other

volunteers. The little garrison numbered only
about one hundred and fifty, all told, and Santa
Anna was soon upon it with an army several thousand strong.

At Refugio Houston succeeded in persuading
most of Johnson's men to leave him, and soon afterwards they joined his own forces. Johnson and
Doctor Grant, another one of the leaders who had
brought contingents for the expedition, went on to
San Patricio with less than one hundred men. A
little later the two detachments were separated, and
first Johnson's party and then Grant's was slaughtered by the Mexicans almost to a man. Johnson
himself, by the rarest good fortune, escaped.

Fannin marched to Goliad, where he had over
four hundred men. On his way thither he had
been elected to command the force. More than
once he declared himself ready to serve under Houston if the latter could only be persuaded to lead the
expedition against Matamoras; but the commander-
in-chief had gone to the east under a commission
from the governor to negotiate a treaty with the
Indians, and Fannin had to act for himself. It was
by this time known that the Mexicans were invading Texas in force, and he awaited them in the
Goliad fortress. About the middle of March he
received orders from Houston, who had meanwhile
resumed his functions as commander-in-chief to
blow up the fortress and fall back to Victoria; but
he had sent out two parties respectively under Captain King and Lieutenant-Colonel Ward, and he

waited three or four days to hear from them. No
news came, and March 19 he started on his retreat. He had gone but a few miles when his force
was surrounded by Mexicans, and a fight ensued
which lasted till night came on. The next morning, seeing himself helpless, Fannin surrendered,
as the survivors among his own men said, with
the agreement that they should be treated as prisoners of war; but Urrea, the Mexican commander,
claimed that it was at discretion. In a few days
Ward's men, who had been captured soon after
Fannin's, were added to the body of prisoners, but
King's had been almost completely massacred.
March 27 the prisoners to the number of three
hundred and seventy-one were marched out under
guard and shot down like cattle in the shambles,
though in the confusion of the slaughter, twenty-
seven of them were fortunate enough to escape. To
give this infernal deed the little palliation that can
be found for it, one must remember that Fannin's
troops were mainly from the United States, and
from the Mexican standpoint were filibusters; but
this fact will scarcely serve to check the reader's
indignation.

From the Alamo Travis made repeated calls for
help, avowing his determination never to give up
the place. On the morning of March 1 thirty-two
men from Gonzales made their way through the
beleaguering Mexicans into the fort, thus swelling
the number of its doomed inmates to one hundred
and eighty-three. As the defense of the Alamo is

I am billing...
or more of...
Santa Anna...
is continued...
cummings...
not lost a man...
has demanded a

with a

receiv

pell

four

If th

mined

Lahi

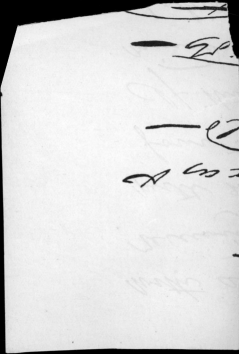

later — The enemy is ...
... inforcements ...
... could intercept to free a
... are in form or friday
call's reply. I send him
... in form myself a ...
... & all like a ...

the most heroic event in American history, so, as
the writer of this volume believes, is the letter in
which Travis announced the opening of the siege
the most heroic document among American historical records.   Therefore to the printed copy which
follows is added a reproduction in which the letter
appears, as nearly as possible, just as it left the
hand that penned it : —

COMMANDANCY OF THE ALAMO,
BEJAR, Feb'y 24th 1836.

To the People of Texas and all Americans in the world.

Fellow citizens and compatriots — I am besieged, by
a thousand or more of the Mexicans under Santa Anna.
I have sustained a continual Bombardment and cannon-
ade for 24 hours and have not lost a man.   The enemy
has demanded a surrender at discretion, otherwise, the
garrison are to be put to the sword, if the fort is taken.
I have answered the demand with a cannon shot, and
our flag still waves proudly from the walls.   *I shall*
never surrender or retreat.   *Then,* I call on you in the
name of Liberty, of patriotism and everything dear to
the American character, to come to our aid with all dispatch.   The enemy is receiving reinforcements daily and
will no doubt increase to three or four thousand in four
or five days.   If this call is neglected, I am determined
to sustain myself as long as possible and die like a soldier who never forgets what is due to his own honor and
that of his country.   VICTORY OR DEATH.

WILLIAM BARRET TRAVIS,
Lt. Col. comdt.

P. S.   The Lord is on our side.   When the enemy
appeared in sight we had not three bushels of corn.   We

have since found in deserted houses 80 or 90 bushels and got into the walls 20 or 30 head of Beeves.

                                        TRAVIS.

Men are often overawed by the storms they conjure up themselves. It was not so with Travis. He had done more, perhaps, than any other man to precipitate the revolution, but he faced its concentrated fury with unwavering courage to the last. Even in the simple "*shall*" of his sentence of self-devotion, whose propriety of diction has been much impeached, there is a calm bow to destiny not yet unveiled that no strenuous "will" could equal in its significance.

The Alamo was besieged from February 23 to March 6, when it was taken by storm. In the early morning the Mexicans, assaulting it simultaneously at three different points, swarmed in through the breaches and over the walls. A desperate hand-to-hand struggle followed, and all but about a half-dozen of the Texans died fighting. Four or five were found after the assault hiding in the rooms of the Alamo, and a Mexican officer begged that their lives might be spared ; but Santa Anna ordered their immediate execution, and they were shot at once. One or two others made desperate but unsuccessful efforts to escape, one of them being captured under a bridge a half hour later and forthwith put to death. Not a man of the garrison was left alive. The only survivors were three women, including Mrs. Almerion Dickinson, the wife of a lieutenant belonging to the garrison, the baby daughter of Mrs. Dickinson, one other child, and a negro boy. The Mexican loss has never been fully ascertained; but an estimate by a cool and careful writer, who based it largely on information from those who took part in the assault, places the number of killed and wounded at about five hundred.

The fourth act of the revolutionary tragedy was now over, and the drama hastened rapidly to a conclusion.

CHAPTER XVIII

THE STRUGGLE FOR INDEPENDENCE

THE convention met according to the call of the council on March 1, 1836, at the town of Washington on the Brazos. It remained in session only seventeen days, but during this time it did notable work. Its most important act was to bring into existence the Republic of Texas, and to give a new direction to the war with Mexico.

In organizing the convention, Richard Ellis, from Pecan Point on Red River, was elected president, and H. S. Kimble secretary. Concerning the membership, it is worthy of note that very few of them had served as delegates to the consultation or the two conventions that had marked the earlier efforts of the colonists to obtain peaceable redress for their grievances. This fact itself helps to show how the conservatives, who had hitherto been trusted and followed, were now losing their hold. Stephen F. Austin was in the United States in the discharge of his duty as commissioner, but Sam Houston was present as a delegate from Refugio. Two prominent members of the council who claimed to have been elected had their seats contested. On account of the contradictory evidence, and the want of time for a new election, an effort was made to have all the claimants seated; but it failed, and the seats in both cases went to the contestants.

That the convention would declare Texas independent was a foregone conclusion. It had become clear that there was no longer any middle ground to take. Whoever may have been to blame for it, the policy of coöperating with the Mexican Liberals had failed; or perhaps it would be more accurate to say, had been thwarted. There was no longer any hope of keeping the war out of Texas, and it was even while the convention sat that the tragedy of the Alamo was enacted and the defense of the frontier broke down. The Anglo-Americans were at length thrown upon their own resources and the help of their friends in the United States. Every reason, both of right and expediency, now called for a declaration of independence, and even the most cautious and scrupulous of the colonists began to consider it as the only alternative. Austin himself, who to the last was keenly sensible of his obligation to Mexico, and whose moral stature and want of fitness for revolutionary leadership were made equally conspicuous by the crisis, was won over. The change in his views seems to have taken place at the time of his passage to the United States in the winter of 1835. In letters written from New Orleans on January 7, 1836, he declared that he had become convinced and was in favor of an immediate declaration. The growth of this conviction was due apparently to the state of public sentiment in New Orleans, which demanded absolute separation from Mexico as the condition for aid for Texas.

Public opinion in Texas, however, was the determining factor with the convention. As already intimated, the feeling had, in the first two months of 1836, become practically unanimous. The growth of it had been vigorous and steady for months before ; and though it had not been powerful enough to control the consultation or the council, it had furnished in a high degree, no doubt, the opposing strength that defeated the execution of their measures. Incident to the social and political organization of the Texas then existing was a strong sense of local independence, and at the same time a great deal of impatience in the separate communities over the want of a united and consistent policy in the face of imminent invasion. This impatience broke forth at Goliad, December 20, 1835, in a declaration signed by ninety-one citizens, which anticipated the act of the convention. How the signers regarded the situation of Texas at the time is best stated in the words of the instrument itself.

It says that —

They [the signers] have seen the enthusiasm and the heroic toils of an army bartered for a capitulation, humiliating in itself, and repugnant in the extreme to the pride and honor of the most lenient, and no sooner framed than evaded or insultingly violated.

They have seen their camp thronged, but too frequently, with those who were more anxious to be served by, than to serve their country — with men more desirous of being honored with command than capable of commanding.

They have seen the energies, the prowess, and the achievements of a band worthy to have stood by Washington and receive command, and worthy to participate of the inheritance of the sons of such a Father, frittered, dissipated, and evaporated away for the want of that energy, union, and decision in council, which, though it must emanate from the many, can only be exercised efficiently when concentrated in a single arm.

They have seen the busy aspirants for office running from the field to the council hall, and from this back to the camp, seeking emolument and not service, and swarming like hungry flies around the body politic.

They have seen the deliberations of the council and the volition of the camp distracted and paralyzed by the interference of an influence anti-patriotic in itself, and too intimately interwoven with the paralyzing policy of the past, to admit the hope of relief from its incorporation with that which can alone avert the evils of the present crisis, and place the affairs of the country beyond the reach of an immediate reaction.

They have witnessed these evils with bitter regrets, with swollen hearts, and indignant bosoms.

The document concludes by declaring the independence of Texas, and the signers express themselves as " relying with our entire confidence upon the coöperation of our fellow citizens." By the end of the next two months all Texas was of the same mind.

So the first work of the convention, after it had

organized, was to appoint a committee to draft a declaration of independence. The next day, March 2, the committee reported, and the report was unanimously adopted. The declaration charged that the Mexican government had broken faith with the colonists by failing to secure them " that constitutional liberty and republican government, to which they had been habituated ; " had " sacrificed [their] welfare to the state of Coahuila ; " had unjustly imprisoned Austin ; had refused to secure trial by jury ; had " failed to establish any public system of education ; " had rendered the military superior to the civil power ; had dissolved the state government by force of arms ; had sought to arrest Texas citizens and carry them to the interior for trial ; had made piratical attacks on Texas commerce ; had denied the Texans freedom of conscience ; had commanded them to give up their arms ; had invaded their country by land and sea ; had excited the Indians against them ; and " had continually exhibited every characteristic of a weak, corrupt, and tyrannical government." Against one or two of these allegations Mexico might have had some defense ; but the indictment was essentially true and proper, and fully justified the assertion of independence.

The convention then addressed itself to the task of framing a constitution. The instrument that was the outcome of their labors was copied in many of its features from the Constitution of the United States, but of course it was necessarily adapted to a single state, and not a federal union. It required congress to introduce by statute the common law, with such modifications as might seem called for, as early as practicable, and provided that the same system should be the rule of decision in all criminal cases. Ministers of the gospel and priests were made ineligible to the presidency or to congress. It was made the duty of congress to provide by law, as soon as circumstances would permit, a general system of education. Persons refusing to participate in the war or aiding the enemy were to lose their rights of citizenship and their land; heads of families were to have each a league and *labor* — in all about forty-six hundred acres — and each single man over seventeen years of age one third of a league; and certain acts of the legislature of Coahuila and Texas passed in the years 1834 and 1835, under which enormous amounts of land in Texas had been improperly disposed of, were nullified.

As to slavery, the constitution provided that persons of color who had been slaves before their immigration to Texas should remain such. Congress was forbidden to pass any law to prevent immigrants from bringing their slaves with them, or to emancipate slaves; nor was any person to be allowed to free his slaves, except by consent of congress, unless he first sent them beyond the limits of the Republic. Free negroes were not to be allowed to live in Texas without the consent of congress, and the African slave trade, or the introduction of negroes except from the United States, was prohibited and declared piracy.

This establishment of slavery in Texas was nothing more nor less than was to have been expected. To judge the act by the prevailing standards of a subsequent age and to condemn it is substantially to condemn the way that nature has of working out its own processes. To the student with genuine historical insight, who takes men as he finds them and seeks an explanation of every movement in a searching analysis of the forces that lie behind it, such reprobation has little significance except as a mark of progress. It easily leads to a complete misunderstanding of the past. It would be idle to suppose that the colonists, the great majority of whom were from slaveholding States, and many of whom had brought their slaves to Texas with them, would not have legalized slavery in framing a constitution. A still greater error has been committed by some in accepting the view that the colonization of Texas and the revolution was the work of the " slavocracy." Naturally enough, the movement resulted in a wide extension of the slaveholding area; but the idea that it was consciously inaugurated and carried out with that object in view is too palpably mistaken to be worth discussion.

Towards the end of the session, the committee on naval affairs, in reporting on a communication from the collector of customs at Velasco relative to the smuggling in of a cargo of slaves by Monroe Edwards, made the following expressions concerning the slave trade : —

Your committee feel bound to give it as their opinion, that the introduction of African Negroes, is in contravention of the existing Treaties between most nations, and the existing laws of this land. And your committee have no hesitancy in stating their views and belief of the extreme impolicy of either covertly or directly countenancing a traffic, which has called forth the indignant condemnation of nearly the whole civilized world. It is to that civilized world that we now, in our present struggle look for sympathy, and hope from that sympathy to extract assistance. . . .

Your committee therefore respectfully suggest that, as a nation just ushered into existence, it most eminently becomes our duty and policy to adapt our measures to the genius and spirit of the age. We must be governed by the opinions of others — we must so regulate our infant steps as to deserve the kind and watchful solicitude of older nations. But while advocating the broad and abstract principle of justice, let us not by taking a retrospective view, of a doubtful and exciting question, interfere with or violate the just rights of our citizens.

What the committee said appears to have struck the convention as worth saying, for an order was passed immediately for the printing of one thousand copies of the report. How these were to be distributed is not shown by the journal, but it is not improbable that a search in the public archives of European nations would bring to light a number of them.

In the course of its labors the convention

adopted various emergency measures for the relief of general or special grievances and for the conduct of the war ; and finally, on the day before its adjournment, it provided for the organization of a provisional government vested with all the powers given to congress by the constitution, except for legislative and judicial acts.   The officers were to be a president, vice-president, attorney-general, and secretaries of state, war, the navy, and the treasury. They were all to be elected by the convention, and a majority of them was to determine any question as to the extent of their powers.   The president was to appoint, with the advice and consent of his cabinet, all officers in public service during the existence of the provisional government ; and that government was specially empowered to borrow one million dollars and pledge the faith and credit of the Republic for its payment, to appropriate the available funds to the defense of the country, and to make treaties with and send commissioners to any foreign power.   David G. Burnet was chosen president, and Lorenzo de Zavala vice-president.

All this work was done in the midst of alarms. The two letters sent out by Travis, respectively on February 23 and 24, had spread the news of the investment of the Alamo, and the convention began its labors with great anxiety for the fate of the little garrison and of the settlements which its capture would lay open to invasion.   March 4 Sam Houston was appointed commander-in-chief of all the Texas troops, regulars, volunteers, and militia. He was to be subject to the general orders of the government *de facto*, pending the election of a president in accordance with the constitution. The day on which this action was taken was Friday, and the convention adjourned that afternoon until the following Monday to give time for the work of the committees; but on Sunday, March 6, it was assembled to hear the reading of the letter sent out by Travis on March 3 — the last before the assault. Houston made a speech relative to his previous course as commander-in-chief, thanked the convention for his reappointment, and left to join the little force that was gathering at Gonzales. It was in the early morning of the same day, as will be remembered, that the storming of the Alamo had taken place, but the news did not reach the convention till the afternoon of the 15th.

Shortly after his departure from Washington, General Houston had sent orders to Fannin at Goliad to march immediately to Cíbolo Creek, east of Béjar, to effect a junction with the troops under himself, the plan being for the united force to march to the relief of Travis and his men; but on reaching Gonzales he found in circulation a rumor that the Alamo had fallen, and he sent further orders to Fannin directing him to fall back to Victoria as soon as practicable. The results of Fannin's tardy efforts to obey this order have already been described.

Houston's arrival at Gonzales was on March 11. He found there three hundred and seventy-four men — trustworthy enough as fighters, but practically without military training. On the 13th Mrs. Dickinson arrived with certain information of the fall of the Alamo and the advance of the Mexicans. A retreat was ordered at once, but before Gonzales was finally abandoned, it was burned to the ground.

Texas is crossed by a number of rivers flowing southeastward, which constituted the best available lines of defense against the invader. Gonzales, then the western outpost of Anglo-American settlement, is situated on the Guadalupe, about sixty miles east of Béjar. The retreat of the Texans which began at this river continued, with various deflections and pauses, for nearly six weeks, gradually converging towards the coast, and finally coming to an end on the San Jacinto, not far from the eastern border of the settlements.

This retreat of course left the settlements defenseless. Under almost any circumstances the prospect of being overrun by an invading army would arouse great uneasiness in a community from which the men have been drained away by the exigencies of war; but the sickening dread that would be inspired by the approach of an army whose reputation had gone before it in such stories as those of Goliad and the Alamo must be left to the imagination. Every human being that could go fled eastward towards the Sabine at once, taking whatever it was possible to carry away on brief notice and with little means of transportation, and the river crossings were soon choked with a throng of terror-stricken fugitives. While the intense apprehension was the worst that the general crowd had to endure, there was no small degree of physical suffering and distress. Children born in a wayside hut or a thicket surrounded by Mexican soldiery became living reminders of the horrors of that flight.

During this time the men who had gathered to the army under Houston were growing constantly more desperate and insubordinate. From the time the retreat began from the Guadalupe until it was renewed at the Colorado his force grew, until it amounted to perhaps fifteen hundred ; [1] but as soon as he began to fall back from the Colorado to the Brazos, the men commenced leaving rapidly. When he reached the Brazos, two companies, one under Mosely Baker and the other under Wily Martin, refused to go farther, and had to be left behind. Baker's company rejoined the main body after it left the Brazos ; but a detachment of two or three hundred, consisting of the sick and inefficient with some guards, was left behind near Harrisburg just previous to the battle of San Jacinto, and the number engaged in the battle was only about eight hundred.

It is not strange, in fact, that the army melted in

[1] There has been much controversy as to the actual number. Houston afterwards put it at only seven hundred ; but the estimates of half a dozen or more of his officers vary from thirteen hundred and sixty to eighteen hundred.

such fashion. Houston kept his plans to himself;
and, though the men were eager to fight, no one
knew when or where the retreat might be expected
to end. They were crazed by the uncertainty and
suspense concerning their families, of whose peril
they were well aware, but of whose fortunes they
knew little ; and in view of their imperfect organization and the want of military discipline among
them, the wonder is that, under such circumstances,
enough of them held together to finish the campaign.
The fact that they did is the best evidence of
Houston's fitness for leadership.

The retreat from Gonzales began on the evening of March 13, and the Colorado was reached
at Burnham's Crossing, near the present site of La
Grange, on the afternoon of the 17th. At that
place a halt of two days was made, after which the
army passed down the east bank of the river to
Beason's Ford, near where the town of Columbus
now stands. There it remained until March 26,
when Houston ordered a retreat to the Brazos.
Meanwhile the Mexican general Sesma had been
dispatched by Santa Anna after the Texans. He
had made his way direct towards Beason's Ford, and
had reached the west bank of the river soon after
Houston had put himself in the way on the other.
Sesma arrived with only a little over seven hundred
men, and the Texans were eager for a fight. Military
critics would probably agree that this was the best
opportunity of the campaign. The Mexican force
in Texas was considerable, but it was in widely

separated divisions. One under General Andrade
had been left at Béjar, one under Colonel Amat was
coming by way of Gonzales to join Sesma, one
under General Gaona was on the march from Béjar
towards Nacogdoches, — being then west of Bastrop
on the Colorado, — and another under General
Urrea was at Victoria. There was nothing to prevent the possible concentration of all these against
the one small army under Houston except a prompt
and decisive blow, such as might have been struck
on the Colorado. Neither could it have been difficult to foresee the demoralization among the troops
and the people at large that further retreat must
bring. But Houston seems to have underestimated
the desperate fighting spirit in his men, and to
have been overcautious about matching them with
regulars. He fell back to San Felipe on the Brazos, and thence up the river about a day's march
to "Groce's," near where has since grown up the
town of Hempstead. It was at San Felipe that
Wily Martin and Mosely Baker refused to retreat
farther, and Baker was left to defend the crossing
there, while Martin was sent to guard that at Fort
Bend, lower down.

At Groce's Houston stopped for two weeks,
which he endeavored to employ in the better organization of his army; but his efforts towards the
development of discipline and *esprit de corps* were
ineffective by reason of the feverish impatience and
anxiety among the men. During the interval Santa
Anna had taken command of Sesma's division on

the Colorado, and had led it straight to the Brazos at San Felipe. There he was checked for several days by Baker's company, but he finally effected a crossing at Fort Bend. He then hurried to Harrisburg and thence to New Washington on Galveston Bay, with the aim of capturing President Burnet and his cabinet. Failing in this, he returned to the San Jacinto River, and there at last, on April 20, he came upon the Texans.

While Houston lay inactive at Groce's, — not having revealed his plans, — with Santa Anna pressing forward and the uneasiness becoming hourly more intense, the provisional government put its hand into the affair. A meeting of the cabinet was held, and it was decided that Rusk, the secretary of war, should go to the army and seek to bring on a battle. President Burnet wrote a sharp letter to Houston telling him that the enemy was laughing him to scorn, that the country expected him to fight, and that he must do so.

April 14 the Texan army left Groce's. The march was first along a route but slightly south of east that might have been followed if the destination had been Nacogdoches, and some have claimed that Houston meant to go in that direction, but the evidence seems to show that he was aiming at Harrisburg from the outset. Only a few miles had been covered when a turn almost due south down the Harrisburg road made it apparent that the retreat had changed to an advance. What was left of Harrisburg — it having been burned by the Mexi-

cans — was reached on the 18th.   Here the sick
and inefficient were left with the baggage under a
guard of seventy-five men, and the army proceeded
down Buffalo Bayou towards the San Jacinto River.
On the morning of the 20th the Mexicans came in
sight, on their march back from New Washington.

During the remainder of the 20th and until the
afternoon of the 21st the opposing forces were
encamped facing each other, the Texans along the
right bank of Buffalo Bayou, and the Mexicans on
the edge of a prairie stretching from the bayou
southward.   On the 20th a skirmish was brought
on by an attempt to capture a piece of artillery
from the Mexicans, but it led to nothing more serious than the wounding of two Texans — one of
them mortally — and two Mexicans.   On the morning of the 21st Cos joined Santa Anna with a reën-
forcement of about four hundred men.   At noon
on that day a council of war was held by Houston,
and it was decided to defer attack till the next
morning; but the men were still anxious to fight
at once, and when their disposition had been ascertained through the officers, he gave the necessary
order.

Nothing further was needed to end the uncertainty and suspense.   What followed was no battle,
but a rout.   The Mexicans were taken by surprise;
and though some of their officers behaved coura-
geously enough, the troops made little resistance.
The Texans charged to the war-cry, " Remember
the Alamo! "   The pent-up fury and the despera-

tion they had been nursing through the memorable six weeks of the retreat beginning at Gonzales came out in one wild burst which did not need a second. Their onset was irresistible, and their vengeance terrible. They lost only two killed and twenty-three wounded, but the scattered and flying Mexicans were shot down like wild beasts, until most of them were finally gathered in one body near night-fall and formally surrendered by Colonel Almonte. Houston reported six hundred and thirty of them killed, two hundred and eight wounded, and seven hundred and thirty captured.[1] Not more than three or four dozen of Santa Anna's army escaped.

Santa Anna himself was captured the next day. Pending negotiations with the provisional government he agreed to order Urrea, who had moved forward and taken Brazoria, to retreat to Victoria, and the other divisions to Béjar. At Velasco, on May 14, he signed two treaties, one open and one secret, by which he agreed to cease hostilities against Texas, to send the Mexican troops out of the country, and to do what he could to secure the recognition of the independence of Texas with boundaries not to reach beyond the Rio Grande. General Filisola, who had succeeded Santa Anna as commander-in-chief of the Mexican forces, ratified the treaty on May 14, and a few days later the last of the invaders had left Texas.

[1] It seems that the wounded were counted also among the prisoners, and that the aggregate should be only thirteen hundred and sixty.

While this campaign was in progress, General Gaines, who was in command of the United States troops at Fort Jesup near Natchitoches, moved up to the Sabine with a large force, and would doubtless have crossed into Texas if he had been able to find occasion; but the Indians were too quiet to justify the step, and it was therefore not taken.

The victory of San Jacinto was followed by a general outburst of rejoicing among the Texans. It was regarded as a great deliverance, and the anniversary of the battle became, in disregard of that of independence, the special holiday of the Republic. Of late years, however, the claims of Independence Day — March 2 — have been recognized, and it is gradually becoming the great red letter day of the Texas calendar.

CHAPTER XIX

HOME AFFAIRS OF THE REPUBLIC

TEXAS can scarcely be said to have had an enviable experience in its essay at independent self-government. During the ten years through which the effort lasted, the young Republic, with small available resources and smaller credit, lived a hand-to-mouth existence and was constantly threatened with bankruptcy. The trouble was heightened by the working of the clause in its constitution which made the president ineligible for a second succeeding term. The result of this was a see-saw policy, each administration reversing, to a greater or less extent, that of the one previous, and neutralizing its work. Every successive attempt to place the financial affairs of the government on a satisfactory basis was a failure, till the wise and stern economy of Houston's second term began to give relief. But during this period the new commonwealth was rapidly acquiring population, wealth, and political experience; and had it continued to stand alone, it would likely soon have become a commanding figure in its rôle of nationality. At any rate, the fair-minded critic will not regard its infant stumblings too severely.

A general election to ratify the constitution and to elect officials for the government thereunder was held in September, 1836. The ratification was unanimous. Houston, Austin, and Henry Smith were candidates for the presidency; but the deliverance wrought for Texas by the battle of San Jacinto had silenced the complaints against the commander-in-chief and made him a popular idol, while the obligations of the Anglo-Americans to Austin were for the moment forgotten. Houston was therefore swept into the presidential chair by a wave of enthusiasm similar to that which had given him the victory in the field. He received over five thousand votes, while Smith had not quite seven hundred and fifty, and Austin less than six hundred. Lamar was elected vice-president; and the new president, anxious that the fierce party strife which had divided the Texans hitherto should now be made to cease if possible, sought to harmonize the factions by appointing Austin secretary of state, and Smith secretary of the treasury.

At the same election two important questions were submitted to the people: whether congress should have power to amend the constitution, and whether annexation to the United States was desired. There were only two hundred and twenty-three votes in favor of congressional constitution mending, and only ninety-one against annexation. In this way the Texans announced at the outset their jealousy of the delegation of sovereign powers, and their clear perception of their true interest and destiny.

Soon after the election congress met and organized the government as adequately as, under the circumstances, it could be done. A seal and standard were adopted, the first being little different from the present official seal of the State, while the second bore a single golden star on an azure ground; but in 1839 the flag was changed to the familiar three bar arrangement, the blue vertical next the staff and bearing one white star, and the red and white of the same size as the blue but horizontal, with the white uppermost. The special feature of the judiciary was that the supreme court was made up of a chief justice and the judges of the district courts, four in number, sitting in banc.

In organizing the new local government the three departments of Béjar, the Brazos, and Nacogdoches, into which Texas had been divided under Mexican rule, were neglected and disappeared; while the Mexican municipalities became the counties of the Republic.

One of the early measures of congress was the increase of the navy. Early in 1836 the Republic had purchased four vessels, which had been employed in patrolling the coast and cutting off the supplies of the Mexicans during Santa Anna's invasion, and had proved themselves quite useful. The Texas government made provision at once for the purchase of additional ships, but they were not delivered until 1839. Long before this the original four were gone, — one sold, one captured, and two wrecked; and for two years Texas was practically without a navy. From 1839 on, the new squadron was put now at one kind of service, now at another, its most important operations being on the coast of Yucatan, which was then in revolt against the central government of Mexico. At length the failure of Commodore Moore, who was in command of the fleet, to obey an order of President Houston's led to a heated controversy between the president and the commodore. In the course of it the Texas congress passed a secret act authorizing the sale of the vessels ; but general opposition among the people prevented the execution of the measure, and about a year later the act was repealed. The Republic held on to its valued treasures of the marine till annexation, when they were passed over to the United States and became a part of its navy.

Of course the army had to be kept up also, for another Mexican invasion might come at any time. Nearly all of the men who had fought under Houston at San Jacinto were settlers, well established in Texas when the revolution began. There were few of these that cared to remain in service when the immediate danger was past, and if they alone had been available it might have been difficult to keep any considerable force in arms at all. But volunteers from the United States poured in, and the army soon rose to more than two thousand. It was a turbulent and troublesome body. When the government appointed General Lamar to take command of it in the summer of 1836, the opposition of the men forced him to retire. Because of this insubordination, and in order to save expense, President Houston wisely furloughed about three fourths of them, and the remainder were put in charge of one thoroughly fit to command, — Albert Sidney Johnston; but his appointment cost him an annoying wound received in a duel with his predecessor, General Felix Huston. The experiences, however, of the government were gradually teaching it; and it soon began to manifest an appreciation of the fact that the most useful branch of its military service was the corps of Indian fighters known as rangers.

This body of troops was organized during the revolutionary period, and it is still in existence. For defense against the Indians, the rangers were especially fitted, and their efficiency for such purposes has been tested over and over again. When the revolution took place, the Indians were still scattered through the country occupied by the whites, and their depredations and outrages were almost constant. This was true during the whole period of the Republic, but gradually the savages disappeared from the interior and the troubles became confined to the frontiers. There, and especially along the northwestern, western, and southwestern borders, they have continued until within comparatively recent years; for the expansion of settlement in those directions has encountered the resistance of the fierce and strong Comanches and Apaches. Early in 1839, in order to protect the exposed districts, the ranger force was greatly strengthened, and the result fully justified the policy.

Houston's policy in dealing with the Indians was friendly and conciliatory, while that of Lamar was hostile and strenuous; but neither could keep them at peace. The conduct of the whites towards them was in general, from the Indian standpoint, highly aggressive and provoked constant retaliation. The Mexicans contributed to the trouble by seeking to incite the Indians to insurrection. In 1838 about three hundred of the Mexican settlers near Nacogdoches were joined by as many Indians in a rising which looked very dangerous for a time; but before any mischief was done the insurgents dispersed to their homes. Their leader, Vicente Córdova, was said to be acting under a commission from the Mexican general Filisola. In 1839 one Manuel Flores, who had made himself conspicuous by trying to stir up the Caddo Indians against the Texans on the eve of the invasion of Santa Anna in 1836, was commissioned as Mexican agent among the Texas Indians by General Canalizo, and was furnished with an elaborate set of instructions to friendly chiefs; but the rashness of Flores brought his enterprise to an untimely — or timely — end. While he was on his way through the country somewhere near San Antonio (Béjar) with a few companions, they murdered several persons; whereupon they were pursued, Flores was killed, and correspondence revealing the scheme was captured.

The most important tribe within the settled area

was that of the Cherokees. These had settled near Nacogdoches on lands granted them by the Spanish authorities, but over which they never enjoyed sovereignty. They had a little share in the Fredonian war. When the revolution came on, there was much fear that they would take part with the Mexicans, and a commission consisting of Sam Houston, John Forbes, and John Cameron was appointed by Governor Smith to effect a treaty with them. This was done early in 1836, but the senate afterwards refused to confirm the treaty. In the summer of 1839, in consequence of the uneasiness produced by the revelations of Flores's mission and similar facts, and of murders charged to the Cherokees, the government decided to expel them. A considerable force was sent against them, and, after a battle in which they lost about one hundred killed and wounded, they were driven out.

The next year came serious trouble with the Comanches. In February of that year, 1840, twelve of their chiefs met commissioners of the Republic in San Antonio to consider a treaty of peace. The Indians refused to surrender a number of white prisoners known to be in their hands, and a company of soldiers was marched into the council chamber, and the chiefs were informed that they would be held until the captives were released. A fight ensued at once in which the chiefs, who were armed, were all killed, and a large number of Indians besides. In revenge the Indians burnt the town of Linnville, and raided the country round that place

and Victoria, killing twenty-one persons; but on
their retreat they encountered a body of Texans,
and were defeated and pursued many miles with
heavy loss. A little later a force of about one
hundred men under Colonel John Moore penetrated to the village of the Comanches and killed
one hundred and twenty-eight of them and captured
thirty-two.

But the most serious matter that occupied the
attention of the Republic was the living problem.
If not rich nor altogether provident, the Texans
were at least big-hearted, and they set up their
national household on a very liberal scale. The
president's salary was fixed at ten thousand dollars
per year, with those of other officials in proportion.
The available resources of the government, however, were small, and the receipts were inadequate
to meet expenses. There was neither much wealth
nor much trade to tax, and if the volume of foreign
traffic had been far greater than it was, Texas could
hardly have been expected to lay a heavy tariff on
it. The ordinary means of raising or anticipating
revenue were rapidly exhausted. Land scrip and
bonds were put on the market in quantities as large
as it would bear, and promissory notes of the government were issued to an extent which necessity
alone could justify.

At the close of Houston's first administration,
at the end of 1838, the total indebtedness of the
Republic was nearly two million dollars, and its
securities were already suffering marked deprecia-

tion. By the end of Lamar's administration, in December, 1841, the debt had risen to nearly seven and a half millions, while the market value of the obligations had fallen to twenty cents or less on the dollar. The severe economy and retrenchment of Houston's second term, 1841–1844, put the finances in much better condition ; but order was not fairly restored until the payment of ten million dollars to Texas by the United States on account of claims surrendered in the Compromise of 1850.

The principal dependence of Texas for revenue was the public domain. This, however, was so vast in its extent that a genuine flood of immigration would have been required to develop its potential value. Then, too, the liberal policy of the government in granting lands so freely to its citizens, especially those who had become such previous to the revolution, necessarily impaired to some extent the demand for what it had to sell. The extensive fraudulent traffic in certificates and claims that prevailed made the matter worse. It was a genuine harvest time for the speculator. Large bodies of land that now have enormous actual value were then secured, sometimes legally and sometimes illegally, for almost nothing. The management of its public domain by the Republic and State of Texas is a subject that tempts the writer on. It cannot be treated adequately in outline, but demands a whole book for itself. There has doubtless been preëminent wisdom in the liberality shown in grants to actual settlers, and in the use of the land for educational purposes; but, on the other hand, the policy pursued has offered many opportunities for private gain at public cost.

The fraudulent land traffic became the occasion, in east Texas, of a local quarrel known as that of the Regulators and Moderators, which began in 1842 and ran through some years. It assumed at one time the proportions of a civil war, and President Houston had to send five hundred men to suppress it. It was not very difficult to induce the forces of the two factions to disperse, but the private feuds born of the affair continued long thereafter.

It is in the educational policy of Texas that the promise and hopefulness of its civilization have been specially manifest. In the convention of 1832 a committee, of which Luke Lessassier of San Felipe was chairman, presented a report recommending a petition to the state government of Coahuila and Texas for a grant of land to Texas " as the foundation of a fund for the future encouragement of Primary Schools." A motion to lay the report on the table indefinitely was beaten by a vote of seventeen to thirty-four, and it was then adopted, apparently without opposition. The State did not make the grant, of course, and it is likely that the writer of the declaration of independence, adopted March 2, 1836, had the petition in mind when he formulated that famous clause in the indictment against Mexico which affirmed that " It had failed to establish any *public system of education*, although

possessed of almost boundless resources (the public domain), and although it is an axiom in political science, that unless a people are educated and
enlightened, it is idle to expect the continuance of
civil liberty or the capacity for self-government."
Evidence is now coming to light to show that the
Mexican government had made some efforts along
the line in which the Texans charged it with failure; nevertheless, it had failed, and this utterance
is notable as showing that the Texans did not
regard the subject with indifference. Further evidence of the fact is found in the constitution shaped
by the same body as that which formulated the
declaration. This constitution required congress
to provide as early as possible for a system of
public education.

To President Lamar it is that Texas owes the
actual provision for the system. In response to a
recommendation in his message to the third congress of the Republic, an act was passed early in
1839 granting three leagues of land to each county
for the support of an academy and fifty leagues for
the "establishment and endowment" of two universities. The work thus begun has been pushed
forward and widened, until the outcome has been
the existing public school system of the State with
the University of Texas at its head.

The real significance of such expressions and
acts by the Texans, and the light they throw on the
nature of the social forces that have been at work
in the making of Texas, may be better appreciated

when it is remembered that the Republic was the
isolated far-away southern outpost of sentiment
in favor of public education.   Unfortunately, the
Civil War set back the fruition of the sentiment
several decades, and it is only a short while that the
State has had an effective system of public schools
at work; but the traditions of Texas have pointed
toward such a result from the very beginnings of
the revolution.   Considering all the conditions
under which the educational policy of President
Lamar was conceived and embodied in legislative
enactments, there is no finer appeal to the noblest
aspirations of a people in history.

The confidence of the Texans of the Republic
in the future of their country is apparent in their
location of its capital.   At the time of the revolution the larger part of the population was settled
below the Old San Antonio Road, between that and
the coast.   The first congress chose Houston, which
had been laid out in 1836 on Buffalo Bayou in the
settled region, as the seat of government till 1840.
But in January, 1839, a bill was passed providing
for the appointment of commissioners to locate the
permanent capital, which was to be between the
Trinity and Colorado rivers above the Old San
Antonio Road.   The commissioners laid out a town
on the north bank of the Colorado at what was then
almost the extreme northwest frontier, but which
is southeast of the geographical centre of the
existing Texas, and of its centre of population as
well.   The new town was named Austin, and the

choice of a site for it was a wise anticipation of growth which the event has fully justified. President Houston, however, claimed that it was too much exposed to Mexican attack to be a safe place for the capital; and in 1842, after the Vasquez raid on San Antonio,[1] he called a special session of congress in Houston. The people of Austin were very indignant, and determined that they would not surrender the archives. A company sent by President Houston succeeded in getting three wagon-loads of matter, but it was followed and forced to bring the books and papers back to Austin, where they were thenceforth kept. The subsequent sessions of the congress of the Republic were held at Washington on the Brazos; but the archives would not go to the government, and the government had finally to return to the archives. The convention to consider the subject of annexation met in Austin, which remained the actual seat of government from that time on.

[1] See p. 246.

CHAPTER XX

FOREIGN AFFAIRS OF THE REPUBLIC

IT can scarcely be said that the new Republic bowed itself into the family of nations with great *éclat*, yet there was evidently a general feeling that its advent was a matter of the gravest importance. For the rest of the world, there were involved in recognizing it, and especially in the establishment of any connection with it, various perplexing problems. Such action would be sure to affect the relations of the country taking it with Mexico on the one hand and the United States on the other. There was an opportunity for England or France to acquire great increase of influence in America by dealing skillfully with Texas, but the chance carried with it the danger of complications that might prove serious. The essential alternatives presented to the United States were either to acquire Texas, or to risk the possibility of its becoming a dangerous instrument of European powers. But the worst feature of the case, for England and for the United States in particular, was that in any attempt to settle upon a policy the irritating question of slavery always thrust itself forward.

As to Mexico, the revolution had already accomplished the severance of Texas from that country, and there was not the remotest likelihood of restoring Mexican sovereignty over the Republic, either peaceably or by force. Of course it was also idle to talk of restoring friendly relations with Texas while the memory of Goliad and the Alamo was so fresh in the minds of the Anglo-Americans. Their vengeance was not satisfied by the slaughter at San Jacinto. It was only the resolute and courageous attitude of President Burnet, backed by the firm support of General Houston, that saved Santa Anna from that vengeance and allowed him to leave the country unharmed. Feeling among the Mexicans was hardly less intense. It was impossible for them to accord respectful treatment to the commissioners that came to Matamoras in the summer of 1836 with a passport from General Filisola to execute certain provisions of the treaty of Velasco. Under such conditions negotiations were useless, not to say impracticable.

To dream of reconquering Texas was still more vain. This, however, the Mexican government refused to admit. It promptly repudiated the treaty of Velasco; and though it was unable to initiate any effective further attacks on Texas, it kept up a series of threats, intrigues with the Indians, and petty raids, whose main result was to nourish an intense irritation among the people at whom they were directed. The treaty was not executed, and the impotent hostilities continued.

The situation might have been worse if the settled areas of the two countries had been actually contiguous; but, as a matter of fact, they were separated from each other by an uninhabited strip spreading northeastward from the Rio Grande and varying in width from about one hundred and twenty miles at the coast to over six hundred at its upper end. This was not easy for hostile armies to cross, and it interfered greatly with retaliatory raiding. In December, 1836, the congress of Texas defined the boundary of the Republic on that side as extending from the mouth of the Rio Grande to its source, and thus including this strip; but neither government established actual jurisdiction over the whole of it. For the time, it did good service to both Texans and Mexicans in keeping them apart.

Rumors sent out by the commissioners at Matamoras, in the summer of 1836, of another Mexican invasion caused great alarm in Texas, but it was not attempted. There was really nothing to fear. The central government of Mexico was then too busy at home to think of measuring arms again with its redoubtable northern enemy. But a counter expedition against Matamoras was planned by the Texans, and a considerable body of troops was gathered at San Patricio in preparation for it. For want of a navy, however, to coöperate by sea, the plan was given up.

For about three years after the campaign ending at San Jacinto, there was no interchange of hostilities between Texas and Mexico worth mention, but in 1839 a number of Texans were tempted to coöperate with the Mexican Federalists in a movement to establish a north Mexican confederation. The Federalists first sought to enlist the help of the Texas government by making, through their leader, General Anaya, certain promises — including probably the recognition of the independence of Texas, in case of the Federalist success — on condition that they should be allowed to transport munitions of war through the territory of the Republic and recruit their forces therein. The proposition was rejected ; but a large number of Texans were induced to assist the Federalists against the Centralists in northern Mexico in two campaigns, one in the latter part of 1839, and one in the summer and fall of 1840. Partly through the incapacity of the Mexican leaders and partly through their treachery, both were ineffectual.

The next year an attempt was made to assert the jurisdiction of Texas over the country east of the upper Rio Grande to which it had laid claim in December, 1836. It took shape in an enterprise whose name might easily be anticipated — the Santa Fé expedition. Santa Fé, the capital of New Mexico, was the one important Mexican settlement east of the Rio Grande in its upper valley, and to get control of it would be practically making good the claims of Texas in that quarter. To be sure it was nearly one thousand miles from Austin on an air line, and much farther by any route it would be practicable to follow, with hundreds of miles of desert to cross in any case ; but President Lamar favored the project, and the disbanding of the regular army in 1841, because of no appropriation for it, provided the necessary material for the organization of a force. Congress refused to pass a bill authorizing the expedition, but the president gave it his approval and sent an official communication to the authorities at Santa Fé in furtherance of its object. He left to them the decision as to whether they should acknowledge the authority of Texas or not, but expressed a desire that there might be a friendly commerce established in any event. In accordance with these expressions, the troops were ordered to be careful, in seeking to establish this authority, not to use force.

The expedition ended most unfortunately. The force numbered two hundred and seventy, and the march was begun near Austin in June. As the party neared Santa Fé at the end of August, the weak and starving condition of the men induced the commander, General Hugh McLeod, to separate it into two divisions, and send the one including those who were strongest in advance, while the other followed slowly. A little more than two weeks later the foremost division was met by a force from Santa Fé, and was induced by treacherous misrepresentations on the part of one of its own number to surrender ; and soon afterwards the remaining body, which was in no condition to

do otherwise, also yielded itself on the promise of
good treatment. The prisoners were all marched
off to Mexico at once and closely confined. In
the spring of the following year the foreign ministers in the city of Mexico secured the release of
such of them as could prove themselves citizens of
the United States or of European nations ; and in
the summer the others also were released, with one
exception. This was the unfortunate José Antonio
Navarro of San Antonio, long known and disliked
by Santa Anna, who was again president of Mexico. Navarro was kept in prison or under surveil-
lance for nearly three years longer, when he at last
managed to escape.

If the opinion of Kendall, member and historian
of the expedition, is correct, the Mexicans at Santa
Fé would have been generally willing to exchange
governments ; but Governor Armijo of New Mexico, who was unwilling to give up the petty absolu-
tism he was enjoying, aroused resistance to the
Texans and defeated their purpose by misrepre-
senting it.

At last the Mexicans decided to take their turn
at the game. On the 5th of March, 1842, General
Vasquez with a force of five hundred men made a
dash at San Antonio and captured the city, which
he held two days. On the same day a small party
of Mexicans occupied Refugio, and two days earlier another detachment had taken Goliad. These
raids aroused great excitement in Texas, and in
ten days there were thirty-five hundred troops in

camp at San Antonio or marching thither. The
Mexicans had in the mean time hurried back
across the Rio Grande. The Texans were anxious
to follow, but they were not equipped for a campaign in an enemy's country, and President Houston informed the commanding general, Somervell,
that such a campaign could not be undertaken in
less than four months. This roused some talk of
an immediate expedition without the sanction of
the president, which led him to issue a proclamation asserting the national character of the war
and the impropriety of such a movement. General Somervell, on reaching the army on March 18,
found the troops so insubordinate that he sought
to turn over the command to the leader they preferred, General Burleson; but Burleson disbanded
them. He could not refrain, however, from pub-
lishing a protest against Houston's opposition to
the invasion of Mexico.

After a short interval came further raids. In
July about seven hundred Mexicans attacked a
body of some two hundred Texans on the Nueces,
but were beaten off. In September General Woll
led another attack on San Antonio. He had about
a thousand men, and again the city was taken, but
not without a fight this time. Twelve Mexicans
were killed and twenty-nine wounded before the
defense was overcome. There was no effort on the
part of the invaders to reëstablish themselves permanently in the old town. Woll stayed only long
enough to be drawn into an engagement with a force

of a little over two hundred Texans that had come
hastily from Gonzales to meet him, in which he lost
nearly one hundred killed and wounded ; but by an
unfortunate mischance he was allowed to strike a
severe blow in return.   A company of fifty-three
men from Fayette County under Captain Nicholas
Dawson that was coming up to reënforce the Texans was surrounded by the Mexicans, who, while
keeping out of rifle range, mowed them down with
grapeshot.   Only fifteen of them escaped death,
and five of these were wounded.   Within two days
after this fight Woll left San Antonio.   He had
come on the 11th of September, and his retreat
began on the 20th.

Again Texas was in a flame of excitement and
anger.   President Houston issued a call for volunteers to rendezvous at San Antonio preparatory to
an invasion of Mexico.   But he ordered General
Somervell, who was then at Matagorda, to take
command, while the troops were clamorous for
Burleson.   At Columbus on the Colorado, Somervell came on a body of two or three hundred men
who were awaiting Burleson, and he disbanded them
and went back to Matagorda himself.   On receiving
further orders, which were sent him October 13, he
proceeded to San Antonio, where he found about
twelve hundred men in several different camps,
poorly equipped, discontented, and disorganized.
His own want of enthusiasm for an invasion of
Mexico was evident, and the force dwindled greatly
before a start was made.   Finally, however, the

march was begun November 18. The number of the men was then seven hundred and fifty. At Laredo two hundred of these abandoned the expedition. Somervell marched thence down the left bank of the Rio Grande till he came opposite the Mexican town of Guerrero. There he crossed over, but soon crossed back and issued an order to return to Gonzales and disband. Six captains with their companies refused to obey the order, notwithstanding which Somervell himself went back with about two hundred men, leaving something more than three hundred to continue the campaign they had declined to abandon.

Those who were left behind organized by electing Colonel William S. Fisher to lead them. They then pushed on down the river to the town of Mier on the right bank, where they got into an engagement with a force of Mexicans six or seven times as large as their own. After inflicting great loss on their enemies they were finally induced to surrender. The number thus made prisoners was nearly two hundred and fifty. These were started to march by way of Matamoras to the city of Mexico. At the hacienda del Salado, about one hundred miles beyond Saltillo, they secured arms by a desperate rush, freed themselves from their guards, and started back to Texas. But after proceeding some distance along the roads they unfortunately took to the mountains, where hunger and thirst soon drove them to despair ; and as soon as they were overtaken they gave themselves up without resistance. They were at once placed in irons and marched back to the hacienda del Salado, where they were forced to cast lots for the selection of one tenth of their number to be executed. The seventeen victims on whom the lot fell were seated upon a log, blindfolded, and shot to death. Most of the survivors were imprisoned in castle Perote. Some of them died there, a few led by General Tom Green escaped, and the rest to the number of one hundred and seven were released by Santa Anna in 1844.

A proposition to Santa Anna emanating from one of the Perote prisoners created for a moment a considerable stir. This man was James W. Robinson, who had been lieutenant-governor of Texas in 1835, and who, after Governor Smith had been deposed by the council, claimed the title of acting governor. The proposition included a plan for a reunion of Texas with Mexico. Robinson was released and sent as a commissioner to present the plan to the Texans. They gave it no consideration, but Robinson obtained his liberty.

One other blow was aimed at Mexico by Texas, but it was warded off by the United States. In the spring of 1843 Colonel Jacob Snively, by authority of the government of the Republic, organized an expedition to intercept a party of Mexican traders returning from Missouri to Santa Fé. Snively camped with one hundred and eighty men on the right bank of the Arkansas River some distance below the crossing of the Santa Fé trail and waited for the traders; but before they came, after he had engaged and defeated some Mexican troops who had come to guard them, his own force was separated by disagreement into two parties, and one of them started home, leaving him with only about one hundred men. When the traders arrived, they were under the protection of about two hundred United States cavalry led by Captain Philip S. Cooke. Captain Cooke gave Snively the rather remarkable information that he was on United States territory, and followed up his statement by taking from the Texans all their guns except ten, which he left them for protection against the Indians. In accordance with an offer he made them, about fifty of the men went back to Missouri with his command and made their way home from there. The others hurried on and joined the division that had previously started back to Texas. The United States afterwards made reparation for this ill-judged act of Captain Cooke to the extent, at least, of paying for the guns he took.

In the summer of 1843 Texas and Mexico were brought by the mediation of England into sufficient accord to agree to a cessation of hostilities until commissioners from the two nations could meet and arrange for an armistice pending negotiations for peace. The commissioners met and agreed to the armistice, but the president refused to ratify the agreement because it referred to Texas as still a part of Mexico, and in June, 1844, Santa Anna sent notice to the Texas government that hostilities were resumed. In point of fact, the further hostile activity of Mexico consisted in massing troops on the Rio Grande and making preparation for the war that was threatened with the United States.

The independence of Texas was no longer really in question. It had been recognized by the United States in March, 1837. France extended her recognition in 1839, Holland and Belgium in 1840, and Great Britain in 1842. As to the possibility of its reconquest and loss of the national status it had gained, that was too slight to be taken seriously into account at all.

It might naturally be supposed that the relations of the Republic with England and France would be quite cordial, and for the most part they were so; but a personal quarrel between the French minister and an Austin hotel-keeper caused a breach with the latter country lasting over a year or two. Of course the radical antislavery element in England, as well as in the United States, had little favor for Texas.

The question of relations with the United States, however, was one of much greater importance; but those relations, while clearly tending to one inevitable result, ran a somewhat fitful and uncertain course. Commissioners were sent by President Burnet to Washington soon after the battle of San Jacinto to secure recognition, proffer annexation, and solicit the good offices of the government in dealing with Mexico. The only outcome of their efforts was the passage of resolutions by the two houses of Congress in favor of recognizing the independence of Texas when she proved herself certainly capable of sustaining it, and the appointment by President Jackson of an agent to visit that country and report on its condition. This agent, Henry M. Morfit, made a report that was none too enthusiastic, and Jackson transmitted it to Congress on December 21, 1836, accompanied by a message recommending the delay of recognition; but, as already stated, favorable action was taken in about two months from the date of the message.

Meanwhile the favor of the administration of President Jackson for Texas had led it to strain its relations of neutrality with Mexico. General Gaines, who was placed in command of the United States troops on the southwestern border of Louisiana early in 1836, and who continued in that office till after the middle of October the same year, was ordered to prevent any crossing of the border by either side; and if in his judgment it should be necessary, he was to anticipate a hostile movement of the Indians by going into Texas as far as Nacogdoches. It was in accordance with these instructions that he was encamped with a considerable force on the left bank of the Sabine when the battle of San Jacinto ended the Mexican advance.[1] He did not enter Texas, because he did not consider that the circumstances under which he was to do so then existed. But in July, on hearing reports that led him to believe an Indian rising near the border was likely to occur, and that a Mexican

[1] See p. 227.

army was about to invade Texas, he sent a detachment that occupied Nacogdoches and remained there some time.

For this act the United States government has been much criticised. The critics, however, have most of them refused to consider both sides of the question. There is not space to discuss it here; but he that is willing to see the strictly technical application of international law yield to the urgent demands of humanity will be very slow to condemn the instructions or the act. What the criticism would have been if the instructions to Gaines had been such as to prevent him from advancing to protect the mass of women and children who fled before the Mexican invasion in March and April, 1836, from the Indian attack that was then feared, can hardly be imagined; and the government may well have been pleased to incur what it did rather than this.

The relations of Texas with the United States, however, turned mainly on the question of annexation, and this will be considered in the next chapter.

CHAPTER XXI

ANNEXATION AND BOUNDARY ADJUSTMENT

THE vote of the Texans in September, 1836, on the question of annexation was practically unanimous; but, tempting as the offer was, it involved too many complications for the United States government to accept it at once. The gravest of these consisted in the vast expansion of slave territory that the acquisition of Texas would bring and the new life it would give to slavery in the United States. The overture came at a time when the issue between the defenders of this institution and its enemies was just beginning to be fierce and irreconcilable. The establishment of William Lloyd Garrison's " Liberator," the Nat Turner insurrection in Virginia, and the inception of the abolition movement coming in quick succession in the early '30's were partly symptoms and partly causes of the growing intensity of feeling on the subject. This feeling, so ominous of sectional division and of civil war, was showing itself in Congress. At the very time when Texas was in the agony of revolution, a struggle between the national representatives of the slaveholding States and those who spoke for the growing spirit of abolition was taking place in the capitol at

Washington. The ground of the contest was shifted from slavery itself to the right of petition, and in the clamors of the dispute that followed, the voice of slaveholding Texas offering annexation was listened to by one party with hesitation and by the other with scorn. The friendship of Jackson could do no more than secure recognition for the new republic, and Van Buren was too wary to commit himself to the policy of annexing it. Not until John Tyler sat in the seat made vacant by the death of William Henry Harrison did the auspicious moment come for a new effort at the consummation of the measure.

Early in the year 1843 the Texas government intimated to that of the United States that overtures for annexation would be favorably received. The news that the subject was being agitated at Washington produced no little uneasiness both in England and in Mexico. In order to avert if possible the acquisition of Texas by the United States, the British *chargés d'affaires* in Texas and in Mexico worked hard to bring about peace between the two countries; but the pride of Mexico still prevented her from accepting the armistice, and the vain negotiations were, as already indicated, followed by a declaration of renewed hostilities in June, 1844. While the negotiations were in progress, in August, 1843, the Mexican government defined its own attitude concerning annexation by announcing that it would regard an act of the United States Congress to that effect as a declaration of war against Mex-

ico. This threat was of small consequence except
in so far as it went to justify the aggressive attitude
of the United States in the war that actually came
a little later. But the part that Great Britain might
be playing in the affairs of Texas was a matter of
much greater importance ; and the fear of a possible danger to American interests growing out of
the relations between those two countries gradually
disseminated itself throughout the Union, and gave
a powerful impulse to the policy of accepting the
gift of Texas proffered by its own people.

The announcement of the Texas government that
it was still not averse to annexation if the United
States would reopen the question led to quiet overtures from President Tyler, which were followed up
until they resulted in a treaty to that end. This
treaty was laid before the Senate in April, 1844.
Had it been fathered by a President less unfortunate in his political relations than Tyler, it might
have been ratified ; but with the solid opposition
of the Whigs, now completely alienated from him,
and only partial support from the Democrats, over
whom he had triumphed in his election, it was defeated by the decisive vote of thirty-five against
and only sixteen for it. The consummation that
the President wished so devoutly was for the time
deferred.

But he had only to wait; the gods were with
him — Jupiter and Minerva, said some, while others
averred that it was only Mars and Mercury, but at
any rate the strongest. He had forced the question

on the politicians in such a way that it became the
principal issue in the next campaign.   True it was
not presented without complications; but taking
into consideration all facts that might account for
the result as not expressive of the popular will
towards Texas, — the unfortunate explanations of
Clay, the defection of the abolitionists from the
Whigs in New York, and what not, — there seems
little room to doubt that the election really turned
upon it.   The Democrats won, and the matter was
practically settled.   The platform of the victorious
party had declared unequivocally for annexation;
its candidate, Polk, had stood firmly and consist-
ently thereon; and when the votes had been counted,
the acquisition of Texas was only a question of
method and of time.

Of a very short time, it proved; but if the friends
of annexation had not changed their method, the
result would have been deferred much longer.   It
would have had to wait, in fact, on the slow and
uncertain process of change in the composition of
the senate, and would probably have not come at
all.   It was clear that no treaty in accordance with
the Democratic policy could command a two thirds
vote of that body; but the triumphant Democracy
was both fearful and impatient of delay.   So the expedient of making the offer to Texas by a joint resolution of the two houses of Congress was adopted.
There was strong opposition to this method among
the senators as unconstitutional, and as involving
a breach of senatorial prerogative; but their objec-

tions were at last sufficiently overcome to secure a
vote for the resolution of twenty-seven to twenty-
five.   The House adopted it as it came from the
Senate by a vote of nearly two thirds.   This was on
February 28.   The next day President Tyler signed
the resolution and thus anticipated Polk in the fruit
of his victory.

The final decision now devolved on Texas.   What
that decision would be must have appeared, to one
. not entirely familiar with the undercurrents of contemporary Texas politics, as dangerously uncertain.
It seemed as though the cautious delay of the
United States government in accepting the Republic's gift of itself might involve the complete loss of
it.   President Anson Jones, who succeeded Houston
in December, 1844, was considered at the time as
opposed to annexation, and in his inaugural address
he avoided all reference to the subject, nor did
the ninth congress of the Republic, whose regular
session ended February 3, 1845, take any action
relative thereto.   But the passage of the joint resolution of the United States congress put a different
face on the matter.   A proclamation was issued by
President Jones on May 5 calling a convention to
pass on the offer, and a special session of the Texas
congress to do the same and also ratify the call.

The president, however, provided two strings for
the Texas bow.   A revolution in Mexico had driven
Santa Anna again from power and placed the government in the hands of the Federalist general José
Joaquin Herrera.   In March, 1845, Ashbel Smith,

the Texas secretary of state, signed the preliminaries of a treaty of peace by which Mexico would recognize the independence of Texas if that Republic would pledge itself against annexation. The treaty was agreed to by the Mexican government in May, and on June 4 President Jones issued a proclamation announcing the cessation of hostilities. Now the congress, which was to meet June 16, had a pair of alternatives ready for its consideration. It could either have peace with Mexico and forego annexation, or it could have annexation and war.

The choice was easy, and it was soon made. On June 21 the senate unanimously rejected the treaty with Mexico. June 23 both houses voted, also unanimously, in favor of annexation. July 4 the convention called for the purpose met and passed an ordinance to that effect. It is said that Richard Bache, a grandson of Benjamin Franklin, who was a delegate from Galveston, voted against the ordinance, but his name appears in the list of those who signed it. The ordinance, together with a constitution framed by the convention, was submitted to the people, and on October 13 both were ratified by a vote that was also nearly unanimous. Whatever uncertainty and hesitation in dealing with the subject there may have been in the United States, Texas knew her own mind, and expressed it with unmistakable emphasis.

It is worthy of note in passing that according to the terms of the resolution by which the United States made the offer, Texas was to retain possession of its public lands.   Thus the State enjoyed the opportunity and was put to the necessity of organizing a system and shaping a policy of management for the vast domain yet remaining in the hands of its government; and no feature of its history is more instructive and more interesting than the development of this policy.

The annexation of Texas without the exclusion of slavery was a severe blow to the radical abolitionists, who advocated the impracticable policy of destroying the institution at once, and it was by no means to the liking of the conservative and growing class, who wished to stop the spread of what they regarded as the social and economic plague spot of the nation.   These constituted at the time a secure majority of the votes of the United States. But it was clear that Texas could not be had except as a slave State.   Imperious and overwhelming natural influences determined this.   Among those, however, who would have barred slavery, if they could, with an iron wall in its existing limits, there were enough who saw the supreme importance of acquiring Texas to turn the scale in favor of accepting it, slavery and all.

As to the war between the United States and Mexico which followed hard upon annexation, that lies mainly beyond the province of this work; but one of the questions connected with it concerned Texas especially, and it demands some attention here.   This is the question relative to the proper boundaries of the Republic.   On the threshold of the discussion, it may be well to say that the too common explanation of the Mexican war as the outcome of a boundary dispute is superficial and misleading. It may be conceded that the attitude of President Polk was more aggressive than that of a chief magistrate backed by the power of a strong nation should have been towards one relatively so weak; but even if chivalry could be expected to control the conduct of governments that are in actually hostile relations, — which it cannot, — it does not follow by any means that the war was, in the essence of the matter, over a disputed boundary. The Mexican congress had asserted that annexation would be regarded as a declaration of war by the United States, and this assertion had never been withdrawn, but had been followed up by the severance of diplomatic relations — the natural preliminary to war. That Mexico was not strong enough to make her threats really dangerous has nothing to do with the technical aspects of the question. As to its moral aspects, if the President deserves any criticism for precipitating the conflict, — and the writer does not think him beyond it, — this is not because the conduct of Mexico, either in diplomacy or war, had until then been such as to challenge the courtesy or forbearance of other nations.

Concerning the boundary, it must be said that Texas as a province or political division of Mexico did not touch the Rio Grande at any point. The line that divided it from the state of Tamaulipas, next the Gulf, was the Nueces. It was separated from Coahuila, further inland, by the Medina, some eighteen miles southwest of San Antonio. Its common boundaries with Chihuahua and New Mexico to the west and northwest were still more remote from the Rio Grande. Even if it be assumed — which can hardly be considered as proved — that the Louisiana Purchase included Texas with its western boundary at that river, this gave the District, Department, or Republic no claim to such a limit after the treaty of 1819. According to the treaty of Velasco made with Santa Anna while he was a prisoner, the Mexican army was to retire beyond that river, and the limits of Texas were not to be fixed west of it; but the obligation of such a treaty has been much impugned. It was agreed to by Filisola, Santa Anna's successor in command, who still had a considerable force under him, and whose ratification should have meant something; but it was repudiated by the Mexican government. The act of the Texas congress passed December 19, 1836, by which it marked out its own limits as at the Rio Grande from its mouth to its source, was in fact no more than a claim to be made good by force. Texas had failed, however, to establish its jurisdiction over such Mexican settlements as lay along that river on its hither side. Therefore President Polk was hardly correct in stating in his message to Congress after Taylor's report of the first skirmish — which took place on the north bank of the Rio Grande near its mouth — that the blood of citizens of the United

States had been shed "on our own soil." But to grant that he was mistaken on this point is by no means the final word as to the ethics of the war.

The conflict could have but one result. Mexico, torn by internal dissension as usual, was unable to gather her strength for a defensive effort, and she was soon overrun. The war cost her not only the strip claimed by Texas between its old provincial boundaries and the Rio Grande, but all the northern part of her dominion, a belt of about ten degrees in width running west from Texas and the line of 1819. Such was the penalty which she paid by the treaty of Guadalupe Hidalgo in 1848 for the pride and want of wisdom which prevented her from forestalling the conflict with an aggressive and powerful neighbor by timely concessions. That she was nominally paid for the territory she lost did little to moderate the bitterness of the compulsion.

The limits of Texas, however, were not yet finally determined. Those which it had laid out for itself by the act of December 19, 1836, — the line of 1819 on the east and north, and on the southwest and west the Rio Grande from its mouth to its source and thence north to latitude 42°, — had been accepted by President Polk and made the basis of his policy at the opening of the war with Mexico, but a convention of the people of New Mexico in October, 1848, adopted an antislavery petition to Congress, in which it protested against the recognition of the Texas claim. The question of the limits of Texas became inseparably bound up with the struggle over the expansion of slavery, which was just about to enter its acute and hopeless stage. Several other questions related in different ways to the same general subject were pressing for answers, and they were gathered in a group and disposed of all together — though in separate bills — by what is known as the Compromise of 1850.

This adjustment cut off about one third of what the Republic had claimed by the statute defining its boundaries. The excised territory included parts now lying in New Mexico, Oklahoma, Kansas, Colorado, and Wyoming. The northern limit given to the State of Texas was the line of the Missouri Compromise. It was anticipated, when the struggle over annexation occurred, that Texas would be cut into several States in order to preserve the balance in the United States senate between the slavery and antislavery interests, and the joint resolution of the congress at Washington by which the offer was made provided that none lying north of the line referred to should be allowed to legalize slavery. Had the occasion to create these new States ever arisen, it would probably have brought serious trouble; but the march of events was too rapid for any such contingency. With the uncertain future then in view, and the heated state of popular feeling that required constant and difficult compromise, it was perhaps a wise precaution that cut off the part from which slavery would have been excluded on organizing it for separate statehood.

The claims of New Mexico were satisfied by giving it the district included between the Rio Grande, the line of 32° north, and that of 103° west. This takes in the capital of the Territory and considerably more than half its area as its boundaries have been finally established.

In payment for this contraction of the boundaries she claimed, and in consideration of ceding to the general government her ships, forts, custom-houses with the revenue therefrom, etc., Texas was to receive from the United States ten millions of five per cent. bonds, half of which were reserved until the holders of Texas bonds should file with the United States government releases from all obligations on account of their claims. The first five millions was paid in 1852. In 1855 the half that had been reserved by the national government, together with two million seven hundred and fifty thousand dollars appropriated to reimburse the State for expenditures for frontier defense, was divided among the holders of Texas obligations who presented them at the Treasury in Washington and signed a release of all claims against the United States. This gave the creditors of Texas about eighty cents on the dollar for the various certificates of indebtedness they held. The Texas legislature had already scaled the debt much more severely, but not all classes of obligations in the same proportion. The act of the United States congress provided that the proposed distribution of the seven million seven hundred and fifty thou-

sand should be ratified by the Texas legislature
before going into effect. The governor of Texas
first submitted the proposition to the people of the
State, who rejected it; but the legislature, which
still did not feel itself precluded from taking up
the subject, was more compliant and approved
the plan. In the distribution the State received
about three hundred thousand dollars which it had
already paid on its debt, and the effect of these
indemnities was to put it in most healthy financial
condition.

One more adjustment fixed the boundaries of
Texas as they now exist, and that was the pre-
cise determination of the line of 1819. The line
as agreed upon by the United States and Spain
was to run up the Sabine River from its mouth
to thirty-two degrees north, thence north to Red
River, thence west to the hundredth meridian, etc.
But Red River has two branches, which join some
distance east of the meridian named, and there
was a question as to which was the main stream.
Texas claimed the north fork; and until the matter was finally adjudicated, exercised jurisdiction
in fact over the district included between the
meridian and the two forks, which was known as
Greer County. In 1896, however, a decree of the
supreme court of the United States fixed the boundary of Texas at the south fork, and the State in
this way lost one of its finest counties.

Yet, while Texas has never relished the loss of
Greer County, the State can scarcely be regarded

as undersized. No other in the Union can approach it in extent of territory. It is also true, in a general sense, that the poorest parts of it are those which have been acquired by the most doubtful claims.

CHAPTER XXII

STATEHOOD

FOR the relinquishment of independence Texas was not without compensation. Her revenue from customs had passed to the United States, but along with it had gone the burden of the diplomatic and military establishments incident to nationality. The payment to Texas provided for by the Compromise of 1850 was partly in the nature of indemnity for the loss incurred by the transfer of the duties; and this, it has been seen, was the main element in bringing order to the finances of the State. The expenditures of the Republic for military purposes had been quite small for some years previous to annexation, but how long they could have remained so if the independent status had continued is exceedingly doubtful. The greatest gain, however, lay in getting rid of the question of foreign relations. Delicate and serious as this question was for the great powers in their dealings with the Republic, it was infinitely more so for the Republic in dealing with them. Now it was definitely settled that Texas should be neither the catspaw nor the *protégé* of England or of France; that she should not be called on to sustain her dignity against overwhelming physical odds ; and that she need not humble herself to obtain the favor of her old enemy Mexico while the asperities engendered by the revolution were yet so fresh. So much of the diplomatic problem as remained was relegated for solution to the government at Washington. What the result was in the case of Mexico has been seen, and it was certainly unfortunate ; but the responsibility does not belong to Texas.

Prosperity soon visited the State. Its abundant natural resources began to make themselves apparent. Immigration flowed in, and wealth began to increase with leaps and bounds prophetic of the extraordinary industrial development of later days. In 1836 the total Anglo-American population of the Republic was probably less than thirty thousand. In 1847, when the first census of the State was taken, the white population was, in round numbers, one hundred thousand, and the number of slaves was thirty-five thousand. The total population in 1850 was about two hundred thousand, and in 1860 about three times as many. The total value of property assessed in 1856 was one hundred and sixty-one million dollars, and in 1857 it was one hundred and eighty-three millions. For the six years from 1852 to 1858 nearly all the taxes collected in the State were given to the counties for local use, the expenses of the state government being paid meanwhile out of the indemnity received from the United States.

In the great stream of immigration that flowed

into Texas during the fifteen years of statehood previous to the Civil War, as well as during the ten years of the Republic, there came a few whose coming was due to the fact that they had committed some offense against the law. It is scarcely worth while to say that there were not enough of this class to determine the character of the population in any given locality; but extravagant stories were told about them, and jokes concerning them were circulated in Texas, and on the outside the stories and jokes were taken quite seriously. In this way the reputation of the State suffered no little, and very unjustly. As a matter of fact it would be hard to find a case in which the reign of law has been so quickly and so firmly established in the midst of frontier conditions.

It was possible for the United States to protect the State from invasion, but Texas had an enemy that was practically within her gates, with whom it was much more difficult to deal. This was the Indian. The tribes inside the limits of the State on the north were friendly, but those of the Indian Territory made frequent raids into the country south of Red River, and were very troublesome. Of course the most annoying Indians, now as of old, were the Comanches, along the western frontier, who liked especially to kill and scalp Mexicans, but were willing on occasion to accept a Texas victim. The interior was protected with tolerable effectiveness from their ravages by the advance line of settlements, yet at no little cost to the settlements themselves. They were the bare hand with which the deadly blows of savagery must be received and warded off. The State employed its ranger force to good advantage, but it is difficult to prevent or anticipate an Indian raid, and the line of exposure was several hundred miles in length.

The circumstances invited the application of the system of colonizing the Indian on reservations. The State granted the necessary lands, and in 1855 two colonies were established on reservations situated the one on the upper course of the Brazos River, and the other on one of its tributaries known as Clear Fork. At the Brazos agency were gathered about eight hundred Indians of various tribes who had long been in contact with the whites, and whose original locations were now within the settled districts, while on the Clear Fork, considerably further west, were placed about three hundred Comanches. The colonies appear, from the reports of the agents, to have prospered beyond reasonable anticipation. The Indians on the reservations, who in 1858 amounted in all to nearly fifteen hundred, were said to be rapidly acquiring the arts of civilized life. A number of them were enlisted in the ranger service and had made themselves very useful. It seemed for a time that the amount expended by the United States government on these Indians, which reached about three hundred and fifty thousand dollars in four years, would be well repaid in tangible good results.

But unfortunately there were on the reservations a few who could not give up the habit of horse-stealing and plundering, and who broke away from time to time and joined with roving Indians, and sometimes white men, in committing depredations. This greatly exasperated the settlers in the neighborhood, who had at best too little patience with the Indians, and they soon began to insist that none of them should leave the reservations at all. In December, 1858, a party from the Brazos reservation which was encamped beyond its limits on the river was surprised by a band of whites and nearly all killed or wounded. The other Indians were much angered by this event and declared their intention to be avenged. The whites made counter threats and organized and armed themselves in anticipation of an outbreak of hostilities. Finally in 1859 the situation became so serious that the Indians were moved across Red River into the Territory. From this time on, the depredations along the northern frontier became specially frequent and troublesome.

Towards the Mexicans remaining within the limits of the Republic the feeling of the Texans was scarcely better than towards the Indians. They were charged with various crimes and wrong-doing, such as stealing horses and exercising a mischievous influence among the slaves. In 1856 a conspiracy among the negroes of Colorado County to rise, massacre their owners, and make their way to Mexico was discovered, and the participants

were severely punished, two being whipped to
death and three hanged; and the Mexicans in that
county, who were said to be generally implicated,
were driven out, as were also those in Matagorda
County. In another notable instance race animos-
ity was reënforced by industrial competition in
such a way as to bring about a series of outrages
known as the "Cart War." This was in 1857. In
that year the Texas teamsters who were engaged
in carrying freight from the coast to San Antonio,
irritated by the success of the Mexican cartmen in
drawing all the business with their profit-killing
rates, began to attack the trains of their unfortunate rivals, kill the drivers, and sometimes even
carry off the valuable freight. This was kept up
until the Mexican minister at Washington addressed a remonstrance to the United States government, saying that seventy-five of the cartmen
had been killed, and many others driven from their
homes. Governor Pease sent a special message to
the legislature recommending remedial measures;
and the matter was taken up by the senate, but
was not pushed to a conclusion. At length, however, when the outrages that had been perpetrated
on the cartmen were extended to the citizens of the
counties where they had occurred, the evil found a
very effective remedy. The citizens began to hang
the perpetrators, and the mischief was soon stopped.

Shortly after this a reign of terror was inaugurated on the lower Rio Grande, from Laredo to
Brownsville, by the Mexican, Juan Cortina. He

began his career by combining with his business of stockman that of cattle-stealer and bandit. In 1859, in order to increase his following, he began to represent himself as the avenger of the wrongs of the native Mexicans, and he had about him at one time five or six hundred of them. In September, 1859, he and his men took temporary possession of Brownsville and killed a peace officer and several other citizens who became involved in resistance to them. Within the next two months two successive expeditions were sent against him, but both retreated without accomplishing anything. In December, however, he was attacked by a combined force of United States regulars and Texas rangers amounting to about three hundred, and was defeated and driven into Tamaulipas.

Such disorders were natural to a new and still unadjusted social organization including diverse and antagonistic elements. There were, however, other activities and tendencies prevailing in the life of the State that were full of promise. One of these appeared in the gradual development of a system of free public education. The provisions of the constitution of 1836 concerning education and the act of January, 1839, in accordance therewith have already been mentioned. This act was followed up by another in February, 1840, providing for a board of school commissioners with power to organize school districts, inspect schools, give certificates to teachers, etc. The educational provisions of the first constitution of the State, adopted

in 1845, showed a distinct improvement over those
of the constitution of 1836 in substituting for the
general and indefinite terms of the latter an
explicit and positive mandate to the legislature to
"establish free schools throughout the State, and
. . . furnish means for their support by taxation
on property." By the same provisions, one tenth
of the annual revenue of the State from taxation
was set aside as a perpetual free school fund, which
was never to be diverted to other uses, and which,
until the legislature should provide for the establishment of the schools, was to remain charged
against the State. The alienation of lands granted
for educational purposes to counties or other political divisions in the State was also forbidden.

The full significance of this feature of the constitution of 1845 could hardly have been understood
at the time, but he that now looks back upon it in
the light of subsequent history can scarcely fail to
see in it a landmark of progress. It was a prophecy
of good that until then had come to no State so far
south. It was the announcement that, in spite of
the social and industrial evils of slavery, Texas was
to set her face towards the rising sun.

The disordered condition of the State's affairs
and the absorption of public interest by the urgent
demands for settlement of boundary and financial
questions operated to prevent action in obedience
to the constitution of 1845 for nearly ten years.
But the Compromise of 1850 and the readjusting
act of the legislature in 1852 brought a little

breathing-spell and a period of relative quiet, in
which there soon came a revival of interest in public education. This expressed itself in the act of
January 31, 1854. The act of 1854 was an elabo-
ration and an improvement of that of 1840. It
set aside as a permanent educational fund two million dollars of the five per cent. bonds received
from the United States, and provided that the interest thereon should be distributed among the
counties in proportion to the number of free white
children between six and sixteen years of age. It
required the division of the counties into school
districts, in each of which the people must provide a good and properly furnished school-building
before they could obtain their share of the public
money. This money was to be expended only in
payment of the teachers, and the balance due, over
and above the amount of the public fund, was to
be paid by the patrons of the school, each contribut-
ing in proportion to the number of pupils he sent
and the time they were in actual attendance.

While this law was crude and imperfect, it offered
a good working basis for the development of a system of public instruction, and during the next few
years there was considerable progress along that
line. The main trouble was that the available
fund was too small, and that it left too much de-
pendent on the uncertain contingency of private
coöperation. In 1860 there were in existence,
under the provisions of this law, about twelve hundred semi-public schools ; but only about one fifth

of the cost of their maintenance was met by public funds. The day of the free school proper in Texas had not yet come.

But the healthy strength of the sentiment in favor of public education is perhaps most strikingly manifest in the measures looking toward the establishment of a state university. The act of 1839, by which fifty leagues of land were appropriated for the purpose of establishing two colleges or universities has already been mentioned. No doubt the reason that two were provided for was that it was considered necessary to have one in the eastern part and one in the western. It was, however, subsequently claimed that the intention of the law was to provide one institution of higher education for men, and another for women. Whatever may have been intended, the idea of having two such colleges or universities was abandoned for that of one, which was on its organization made coeducational. The act of February 11, 1858, was a more definite step towards realizing the plan of a state university. This provided for the creation of an endowment for an institution of higher learning by setting apart for the purpose one hundred thousand dollars of the United States bonds in the treasury, and every tenth of the alternate sections of land reserved by the State in the grants to railroads made in pursuance of the statute of January 30, 1854. The statute referred to granted sixteen sections of land for each mile of railroad to be built thereafter in the State, the land to be surveyed in

solid blocks, and alternate sections to be reserved
by the State. The act of 1858 provided also for
the organization of the university, but this was prevented by the approach and outbreak of the Civil
War.

In politics Texas was rather slow in adapting
itself to party alignment on national issues. Relative to the questions growing out of the Mexican
war and to most of those involved in the Compromise of 1850, there could be, in the nature of the
case, but one party in the State. The contests
were, therefore, of a personal nature, and the elections decided between men rather than policies.
So long as this was true, the sympathies and antipathies of the revolutionary and republican periods
were constantly revived and emphasized. They
were thus prolonged beyond their natural term, and
served greatly to intensify and usually to embitter
personal and political relations. As late as 1859
General Houston thought it worth while to reply
on the floor of the United States senate to what
he regarded as criticisms on his management of the
campaign of 1836, which had just been published in
Texas, and by this means to invite further acrimo-
nious attacks upon himself. But gradually the
momentous questions of national policy claimed the
attention of the Texans, and parties began to form.
For this movement also the ground was cleared by
the Compromise of 1850 and the financial readjustment of 1852. Excitement over national issues
began to appear in Texas during the struggle in

congress over the Kansas-Nebraska bill, which was
favored by Senator Rusk and opposed by Senator
Houston.   Houston's opposition to the bill cost
him, for the time, much of his popularity in Texas;
but he was never the man to bow before a political storm.   The first strong wave, however, from
the centres of national politics that swept over
Texas was that of Know-nothingism.   In 1855 the
Know-nothing party elected one of the two congressmen from Texas and also cast a surprisingly
large vote for its candidate for governor, but the
existence of the party was as brief in the Southwest
as in other parts of the Union.   By 1857 Texas
was so Democratic that Hardin R. Runnels, the candidate of that party, was able to beat Sam Houston, who was supported by the elements opposed
to it, for governor by a majority of about nine
thousand in a total vote of only a little over fifty-
five thousand.   This was the Texas vote of censure
on Houston for his attitude towards the Kansas-
Nebraska bill; but the State could not withdraw
its favor permanently from the man to whom it
owed so much, and two years later he turned the
tables by running as an independent for the same
office and beating Runnels, who was again the candidate of the Democracy, in nearly the same proportion.   The result, however, was not due simply
to the revival of Houston's popularity.   The more
radical Democratic leaders favored the reëstablish-
ment of the slave trade, to which Texas was strongly
opposed; and while their views were not adopted

by the party, their utterances cost it many a vote.
Around Houston, on the other hand, rallied the
conservative element, with its dislike of extreme
policies, its love of the Union, and its instinctive
dread of civil war. This must be considered in
accounting for the change of nearly ten thousand
voters from the alignment of 1857. The State had
again passed censure, but this time it was on the
fire-eating section of the Democracy.

CHAPTER XXIII

CIVIL WAR AND RECONSTRUCTION

IF that country only is happy whose annals are uninteresting, happiness is not for Texas. Her people have never sunk into the inert obedience to circumstances that takes the life out of history. They have usually been impulsive, but never passive. The thoughtful historian, however, will not accept the principle of the aphorism. Intense experience and forceful reaction are the price of character, as well in the collective as in the individual life. Texas has had her share of such experience; and the reaction, whether rightly directed or not, has always been strong. Her most hopeful traits are abounding energy and vitality. Where these exist, knowledge comes, and wisdom follows in due time. But it is folly to judge the conduct of states by the standards of personal morality, or to expect of a commonwealth the intelligent utilitarianism that should be manifest in the better coördinated and controlled life of the individual. In public action the immediate working of the economic, the racial, or the traditional motive is necessarily more evident than in the behavior of the private citizen; nor is it worth while to look for fine ethical influences

behind constitutions, statutes, or party platforms.
While these influences grow and strengthen with
the progress of civilization, we have unfortunately
not yet come to where they usually determine politics.

This is said, not simply by the way, but in explanation of what is to follow. It gives the point
of view from which alone the conduct of Texas
during the period now to be taken up can be understood. The same " ordinance of nature " which
Daniel Webster claimed had excluded slavery from
New Mexico had fixed it upon Texas. Then, too,
eagerly as the people of Texas had turned from
Mexico to merge again with those of their own blood
and institutions in the United States, and warmly
as they loved the Union, out of their political experience and traditions they had inherited a still
stronger sentiment of particular attachment to the
State. It was, therefore, but natural that they
should be drawn into the general current of secession which swept through the Southern States in
the early '60's.

So it proved, in spite of certain appearances to
the contrary as the crisis approached. The election
of Houston in 1859 was, in a considerable measure,
a victory for the conservative Union-loving element
over the more radical portion of the Democracy.
But already the course of events, throughout the
United States, was passing beyond the control of
the leaders. Efforts to enforce the Fugitive Slave
Law and resistance thereto, together with the John

Brown raid, had so exasperated the people both
North and South that it was now impossible to
calm their rising passion or to compromise further.
The election of Lincoln to the presidency in 1860
brought the culmination of sectional differences.
South Carolina led the way in seceding from the
Union, December 20, 1860, and within a little over
a month Georgia and all the Gulf States to the east
of Texas followed the example.

Meanwhile Governor Houston, like Daniel Webster in the days when the operation of the Compromise of 1850 — especially the Fugitive Slave Law —
was rousing furious agitation among his constitu-
ents, had centred all his strength in the vain effort
to allay the feelings of his people and divert them
from their object. With a more aggressive way
and less of facile persuasiveness than Webster, he
was still a man of powerful influence on the platform, and he might have accomplished anything
less than the impossible ; but this was the task, in
fact, that he had now set himself, and it is no wonder that he failed. In Texas almost the entire vote
in the presidential election of 1860 was divided
between Breckinridge and Bell. The conservatives
and opposers of secession rallied to the support of
Bell, and what Houston could do for them was done.
He was outspoken in his condemnation of the dis-
unionists and his claim that the success of Lincoln
would not justify secession. The utterances of the
Breckinridge men were exactly to the contrary on
both points. The issue was fairly made, and the

result was a crushing defeat for the conservatives. The Breckinridge electors received more than forty-seven thousand votes, while those for Bell had only a little over fifteen thousand.   Houston no longer had Texas at his back.

Nevertheless he did not despair.   In spite of repeated and urgent petitions and requests that poured in upon him, he refused to convene the legislature to call a convention until a number of political leaders had taken the extra-legal step of issuing the call.   This was done on December 3, 1860, and the time appointed for the convention was January 28, 1861.   December 7 Houston issued a proclamation calling an extra session of the legislature to meet January 21.   Meanwhile, in pursuance of a joint resolution passed by the legislature February 16, 1858, growing out of the Kansas troubles and providing for a call by Texas under certain contingencies of a convention of the Southern States for the preservation of their equal rights, he had sent a circular letter to the governor of those States proposing such a convention.   The letter seems to have been neglected; at any rate, there was apparently no action in response to it.   This proposition, as well as the call for the extra session of the legislature, was doubtless intended to avert or forestall the much dreaded act of secession.

But the tide was now too strong to turn or check. The legislature met on the day appointed, and the governor laid before it an earnest and strong message deploring the election of Lincoln, but reiterat-

ing his belief that it did not demand secession;
recalling the obligations that Texas had incurred to
the " border States " [1] during the revolution; favor-
ing coöperation with the other States of the South
and the submission of any final measure to a popular vote; and urging caution and moderation. The
views and most of the suggestions of the governor
met with little favor. The legislature immediately
repealed the joint resolution of February 16, 1858,
under which he had acted in proposing a convention
of the Southern States for coöperation in preserving
their equal rights in the Union. Then by a large
majority it recognized the convention that had been
called to meet January 28 as empowered to act for
the people, requiring only that its action should be
submitted to them.

The convention met in accordance with the call,
organized with Judge O. M. Roberts as chairman,
and established at once official communication with
the governor through a committee. He assured
the convention of his obedience to the will of the
people, asserting that as of old he was with his
country. On February 1 an ordinance of secession
was passed by a vote of one hundred and sixty-six
to seven. The ordinance was to be voted on by
the people February 23. The convention, anticipating popular ratification of the ordinance, provided for the election of delegates from Texas to
join with those of the other seceding States in es-

[1] That is, those slave States that were adjacent to the free
States.

tablishing a provisional confederate government at
Montgomery, and for the appointment of a committee of safety. After a short session it adjourned
to meet again on March 2, by which time it was
expected that the result of the popular vote would
be known.

At the appointed time the convention reassem-
bled, and on March 4, the day of Lincoln's inau-
guration, it counted the vote — over forty-four thousand in favor of secession, and a few more than
thirteen thousand against it.

The State had broken finally away from Houston's lead, but during the canvass he had put himself on record in public utterances that came as
from the tongue of a prophet. In a speech at
Galveston a few days before the election, he stood
in the presence of a crowd to whom few others
could safely have spoken as he did, and, deprecat-
ing the resistless impulse that was hurrying them
on to secession, he prophesied for the South ultimate defeat. At the same time he declared his
sympathy for the State and his determination to
stand by it, "right or wrong." A few weeks later
his last act of opposition to the policy which was
approved by the people and on which the leaders
were now determined cost him his official life. On
being summoned to appear before the convention
on March 16 and publicly take an oath of office by
which he must swear allegiance to the Confederate
States, he refused, and challenged the right of the
convention to exist after it had performed the func-

tion of submitting the ordinance of secession to the people. Thereupon it declared the governorship vacant and directed the lieutenant-governor, Edward Clark, to assume the duties of the office till the next election. An effort was made by Houston's friends in the legislature to secure interference in his favor by that body, but it failed. He then retired to his home in Huntsville, where he remained till his death in 1863.

The war was soon under way; but, fortunately for Texas, that State never became the scene of active military operations. The Texans poured forth to join the Confederate armies, and some of their organizations, such as Hood's brigade and the Terry rangers, won proud eminence on many a bloody field; but their record was made in other States. The committee of safety provided for by the convention organized the defense of Texas, appointing Colonel Ben McCulloch to take charge of the post at San Antonio, Colonel Henry E. McCulloch to command the forces on the northwestern frontier, and Colonel John S. Ford to command those on the Rio Grande. It also sent commissioners to confer with General Twiggs, who was in command of the Federal troops in Texas, relative to the surrender of his men and of the property of the national government in his charge. Twiggs was a Southern man and a sympathizer with secession. He promised to surrender after a show of force had been made, and so he did. The troops were to be allowed to leave the State, taking their arms. The property and munitions of war given up amounted in value to twelve hundred thousand dollars.

This advantage was followed up by an effort to secure control of New Mexico. In the summer of 1861 the Confederates under Lieutenant-Colonel John R. Baylor obtained a lodgment on the Rio Grande in the southern part of the Territory and captured seven hundred Federals who marched against them. Early the next year the campaign in that quarter was renewed by General Sibley of the Confederate army, who defeated the Federals under General Canby at Val Verde. The Confederates then pushed on and occupied Albuquerque and Santa Fé; but their advance was checked at Apache Cañon near Santa Fé, and after that they gradually retired. They abandoned the Territory finally in July, 1862.

The defense of the Texas borders was sufficiently effective to keep the Federal troops from penetrating into the State until the war was over. In the fall and winter of 1862 Galveston was in their possession for nearly three months; but at the end of that time it was recaptured, and thenceforth it remained in the hands of the Confederates. In September, 1863, the Federal general Banks tried to break in by way of Sabine Pass, but his effort ended in a disastrous defeat. In the fall and winter of 1863–1864 he got possession of almost the entire coast line except at Galveston and the mouth of the Brazos, but he held it for only a short time.

Finally, in March, 1864, he made, in coöperation with General Steele, an attempt to advance up Red River and capture Shreveport and enter Texas that way, but a decisive defeat at Sabine Cross Roads[1] drove Banks back to Alexandria and Steele to Little Rock. There was no fighting in the interior of Texas during the whole period of the war, but it is a fact worth noting by the curious that the last engagement between the Federal and the Confederate forces took place at Palmito near Palo Alto on the Rio Grande, May 13, 1865.[2] The number of men engaged was only a few hundred on each side, but the fighting was energetic, and the casualties relatively numerous. The Federals were forced to retreat ; the results, however, were of no importance. It was simply the final sword-thrust of the dying Confederacy.

Texas suffered little by the war except for the drain upon the strength of its citizenship and upon its material resources, and the latter were recruited in ways not possible for the other Confederate States. It was the only one of them that was not overrun by invasion. Crops were planted and gathered while the conflict was in progress, and business went on with a degree of security and regularity that prevailed nowhere else in the South. The line of the Rio Grande was the one border of

---

[1] The battle is known in Texas as that of Mansfield.

[2] The place was almost the exact spot where the Mexican war began. The time was more than a month after the surrender at Appomattox.

the Confederacy that could be neither blockaded nor controlled by Northern armies. It was more or less infested by robbers, and there were one or two raids up the river by the Federal troops in the course of the war, but there was no effective interference with the commerce back and forth across the river. As much of the cotton raised in Texas as could escape the State and Confederate tax-gatherers might pass out through the wide gap freely, and a great deal did go that way; but the means of transportation were so inadequate and costly that the trade was greatly handicapped. On the whole, Texas saw little of the worst actualities of the war as they appeared in the States where the hostile armies met and struggled, and when it was over she was soon ready to begin anew the march of intellectual and material progress.

But before the energies of the Texans could be fairly turned again to the industrial and educational affairs from which they had been diverted by the war, there was set a task for them which it required all their strength and patience to accomplish. This was to save the State from the mischievous effects of the congressional policy of reconstruction. It would no doubt be as much a mistake to question the sincerity of those who were responsible for the policy as it would be to impute bad motives to the Southern people in seceding; yet it will now be denied by few that the majority in Congress acted with undue haste and with too little appreciation of real conditions in the South. Naturally there was considerable friction between the emancipated slaves and their old masters, nor was it to be expected that they would always show mutual forbearance in dealing with each other. There were grave problems concerning the adjustment of their relations, which still exist and clamor for solution; but the solution, if it come at all, must come from the people of the South themselves. The efforts of others, however well meant, have served in general only to add complications. This fact has been sharply driven in upon the national intellect and conscience by the experiences of the reconstruction epoch.

The first organization of the Texas government took place under President Johnson's plan of reconstruction. On June 17, 1865, the President appointed A. J. Hamilton provisional governor. Hamilton had been prominent in the politics of the State before the war; had been a member of Congress when secession took place and had refused to resign; and had been a brigadier-general in the Federal army and military governor of Texas by appointment of President Lincoln in 1862. Towards the end of July, 1865, he arrived in Texas and began his work. Meanwhile, on June 19, General Gordon Granger, of the United States army, had taken military possession of the State, and had issued a proclamation declaring all acts of its government subsequent to secession illegal, and the negroes free. Governor Hamilton issued a proclamation to the negroes, who had now been released from slavery by the thirteenth amendment to the United States constitution, informing them that the government could give them nothing, and advising them to go to work for themselves. He then called a convention to provide for the reorganization of the government. Those who had supported the Confederacy qualified as voters at the election of delegates by taking the oath of allegiance to the United States government.

The convention adopted the constitution in force in the State before secession, with amendments made necessary by the outcome of the war, recognizing the abolition of slavery, renouncing the right of secession, conferring certain civil rights on freedmen, repudiating the debt incurred by the State in waging the war, and assuming the tax that had been levied by the United States government on Texas from the time the State had seceded. The revised constitution was submitted to the people and ratified by them, and on the same day was held a general election in which J. W. Throckmorton, one of the seven who had voted against the secession ordinance of 1861, was elected governor.

The new government bent its energies at once to the restoration of order and the improvement, so far as lay in its power, of the general condition of the State. This was no easy task. While the feeling left in Texas by the war was perhaps less bitter than in the States that had suffered more, it was sufficiently intense, for the time, to be dangerous for an unpopular official, or for the man whose duty required him to execute an unpopular law. Nevertheless, though the Texans were too strong in their convictions and too stalwart in character to yield with docile readiness to the painful process of social and political readjustment, they had too much good sense and self-control to continue the vain struggle when a better day was already in sight. It was therefore unfortunate that their work was interfered with by a further test of their capacity for endurance; but so it happened.

Congress refused to accept the results attained under the presidential plan of reconstruction, and decided that the work must be done over according to its acts of March 2, March 23, and July 19, 1867. These acts provided for a new reorganization of the governments of the Southern States in which the negroes should participate, but those who had taken an official oath to support the constitution of the United States, and had afterwards engaged in the war of secession, should have no share. The legislatures of the reorganized governments were to adopt the fourteenth amendment to the constitution of the United States, which had been proposed by Congress, and had already been rejected by most of the Southern States. Until the new governments were formed and approved by Congress, the South was to be under military rule. It was divided into five districts, one of which was composed of Louisiana and Texas, and the general in charge of this district was Sheridan.

General Sheridan at once inaugurated a severe and radical policy in crushing out the alleged disloyalty in the State. Governor Throckmorton was removed as an "impediment to reconstruction," and the great body of state and local officials gradually shared his fate, their places being taken by men who were expected to be strenuous in carrying out the congressional policy. The result was that the government fell into the hands of a few men, who were out of sympathy with the great mass of intelligent and influential citizens. They had the almighty support of the United States troops, together with such backing as could be given them by the mass of negroes, a number of whites who became Republicans for money's sake, and some others — in the main excellent men — who were Republicans by conviction. What the working of such a government would be can easily be imagined. But even the outlines of the picture would be incomplete without some notice of the irritation produced by the interference of the officials of the Freedman's Bureau on behalf of the negroes against the whites. This, to the Northern man who saw the situation from a distance and understood neither the Southern white nor the negro, may have appeared necessary to protect the blacks ; but its practical working was to cut them off from their old masters, on whom they must ultimately depend for employment.

The work of congressional reconstruction covered about three years. In 1868 a new convention was

elected in accordance with the terms of the act of
Congress. It shaped a constitution which was submitted to the people and adopted in November,
1869. At the same time state officers and congressmen were elected. At its session beginning
February 8, 1870, the legislature ratified the thirteenth and fourteenth amendments, and elected
United States senators. On March 30 Texas was
"readmitted" to the Union, and on the 31st her
senators and representatives took their seats. The
troops which were distributed through the State
were withdrawn, and the bitter trial of reconstruction was over.

The government which the congressional policy
had entailed upon the people of Texas was one for
which they had little love. At the election that
took place in November, 1872, the Democrats
secured control of the legislature and filled all the
seats belonging to the State in congress; but the
governor, E. J. Davis, had been chosen for a four
years' term. In December, 1873, Democratic victory at the polls made Richard Coke governor;
Davis, however, disputed the constitutionality of
the law under which the election had been held
and refused to surrender the government. Both
sides were backed by military force, and it looked
for a time as if the dispute must end in bloodshed;
but on the refusal of President Grant to support
Davis with troops, the opposition dissolved early
in January, 1874, and Coke and the various officers of his administration were installed without

farther trouble. In 1876 a new constitution was adopted in place of that formed under the reconstruction act, and the State had finally rid itself, so far as it could, of whatever might remind it of the darkest period in its history.

CHAPTER XXIV

THE TEXAS OF TO-DAY

RID of the incubus of slavery, and with her government again in the hands of her own people, Texas received a new progressive impulse that has seemed to grow and strengthen with each succeeding year. It would appear as if the industrial and moral energies of the State were emancipated along with the slaves, and the record of its development during the last quarter of a century has been really wonderful. In population, in wealth, in education, and in general culture, the increase has been equally striking. The grain of Anglo-American mustard seed planted in the far Southwest has grown to a stately tree, in which many of the best ideas and impulses of the whole outer world have come to nest.

This is no idle boast, but the statement of a fact. The greatness of Texas lies not so much in its vast extent of territory and its abundance of natural resources as in the character of its people, which is a composite — with the good predominant — of qualities peculiar to many lands, whence the citizenship of the State has been recruited.

As to the territorial extent of Texas, there is

undoubtedly a degree of instructiveness in the comparisons which its patriotic citizens so often make by superposing it as a measure on other political divisions of America or Europe and thus emphasizing its enormous area and showing how small New England or even Old England or France appears relative thereto ; but such comparisons suggest to the economist and the historian of real insight facts that are far more important. Of much greater significance than mere reach of surface is the extreme productiveness and widely varying adaptability of the land. These constitute the natural basis for a complex and highly developed civilization ; and they promise for Texas, in spite of the swift advance of industrial centralization that exploits every gift of nature for the benefit of distant commercial centres, a preëminence of strength and influence that is as yet scarcely foreshadowed.

In its agricultural resources Texas can hardly be said to have a rival. In a wide belt extending into the State from the north for the greater part of its length is one of the finest bodies of tillable land that are to be found in the world, the soil being black, deep, and exceedingly rich. The staple crops grown thereon are Indian corn and cotton ; and the yield, when climatic conditions are not too unfavorable, is in overflowing abundance. Equally productive are the river bottoms eastward from this belt. On the lower course of the Brazos much sugar is produced. Stretching along the Gulf coast is an almost level plain from fifty to one hundred miles in width which is specially adapted to the growth of vegetables and fruit, and in the north-eastern end of it the production of rice is becoming very extensive; while in the sandy or red soils of eastern Texas appears an even greater fitness for the cultivation of many varieties of fruit.

Certain facts indicated by the Twelfth Census bring into strong relief the importance of the agricultural interests of Texas. The statistical tables show that in 1899 this State produced more than twice as much cotton, which is its staple crop, as any other, and more than one fourth of the entire crop of the United States. The value of the Texas product for that year was nearly one hundred million dollars. There were in 1899 only four States of the Union that surpassed Texas in the gross value of their agricultural produce, and it seems well assured that these four must soon be outstripped in the unequal race.

While Texas is thus far mainly an agricultural State, and while it will perhaps be such for some years hence, it is not for tilling the soil alone that nature has given it advantages. The southwestern and western parts of it are too dry for agriculture without irrigation, but they afford excellent pasturage for large herds of cattle. East Texas has immense forests of pine and other valuable timber. The mining interests of the State are already of considerable importance, but there seems good reason to believe that hardly a beginning has been made in the development of its mineral resources. The precious metals have been found in paying quantities in the central mineral region of the State and in the Trans-Pecos district. In the former and in eastern Texas are fine deposits of iron ore. Many thousand square miles of the territory of the State are underlaid with coal and lignite beds, and at Beaumont and Corsicana are highly valuable oil wells.

As to the Texas cattle industry, again the statistics afford the clearest light. In the value of its domestic animals in the year 1900, this State was far ahead of all others except Iowa, which surpassed it slightly, but was evidently about to be overtaken. In the value of its neat cattle, Texas was already well in the lead of all the other States.

In manufactures, the State of Texas is yet far behind, and in fact it can scarcely be said to have even entered the race. During the decade from 1890 to 1900 it did no more than to rise from the twenty-fourth place among the States and Territories, with an annual product of about seventy millions in value, to the twenty-third, with a product valued at nearly one hundred and twenty millions. But while there are certain obstacles to the development of manufacturing industries in Texas, as for example in the want of skilled labor and the ancient difficulty in producing iron of getting the fuel and the ore together, it seems impossible, when one takes into consideration the abundance and variety of raw materials and the generally favorable conditions in other respects for manufacturing in the State, that it should not soon forge ahead along this line, as it is doing so rapidly in others. This has been prevented hitherto, in large measure, by the scarcity of capital in the Southwest, and the ease of profitable investments without the risk attendant upon the establishment of new industries. But the available capital in this State is increasing, and rates of interest are falling so rapidly that unemployed money must soon be driven towards manufacturing channels. There seems to be at present a strong drift towards the development of textile industries in Texas, and it is likely that the first great impulse will come from that direction, just as it has in other States of the South.

From whatever quarter it may come, however, the impulse will be welcome. It is to be hoped that Texas is meanwhile acquiring the rightness and strength of habit that will enable her to deal successfully with the grave political and social problems of a more complex industrial system, but the delay should not be over-long. The mere art of money-making is undoubtedly too much sought after by this generation. Education and experience must gradually give to the genius of American civilization a healthier view of the significance and uses of life which shall regard wealth less as an end and more as a means than now; but wealth must remain, as society is at present organized, the most abounding source of individual and national influence. From this standpoint, it is a less important fact, in measuring the relative advantages of the largest and smallest States in the Union, that Rhode Island has as many senators at Washington as Texas, than that the income per capita of her population from agriculture and manufactures combined is over four hundred and forty dollars per annum, while that of the people of Texas is less than one hundred and twenty.

One standard by which the progress of a people may be measured with substantially fair results is the means of intercommunication. A few statements will suffice to show the advantages that Texas now has in this respect, and how they have come. Railroad building in the State began in 1852 with the Buffalo Bayou, Brazos, and Colorado Railroad, which was started west from the town of Harrisburg in that year, and which was the germ of the great Sunset system of to-day. The next road was the Galveston and Red River, begun at Houston in 1853 with the plan of crossing the State towards the north. The name of this road was changed in 1856 to the Houston and Texas Central. The coming of the Civil War practically stopped railroad building, nor did it begin again actively till near the close of the reconstruction period. In 1870 the State had in operation only about five hundred miles of railway, or about one mile for every five hundred and forty square miles of territory; but from that time forward the mileage increased with extraordinary rapidity. The Houston and Texas Central was pushed northwards across the State, with branches diverging in various directions, the

Texas Pacific westward across the northern portion from the eastern boundary to El Paso; the International and Great Northern southwestward from the connections afforded by the Texas Pacific at Longview to Laredo on the Mexican border, whence the Mexican National soon afforded passage to the city of Mexico; and the Galveston, Harrisburg, and San Antonio, which was simply a new name for the old Buffalo Bayou, Brazos, and Colorado line, west through San Antonio to the Mexican border at Eagle Pass, whence connection with the city of Mexico was supplied by the Mexican International, and northwestward up the Rio Grande to El Paso, whence the Southern Pacific opened the way to California. In 1876 the lines in operation in the State aggregated two thousand miles, or about one to one hundred and thirty-two square miles of the State's surface. In 1890 the figures had so changed that the aggregate mileage reached more than eighty-seven hundred, while the ratio was a little over one to thirty-two. The corresponding figures for the State of Massachusetts the same year are a little above two thousand, and something over one to four. In 1900 the total mileage in Texas was something over ten thousand. Illinois and Pennsylvania had each a little more. The ratio of miles of railway to square miles of area in Texas had risen to one to about twenty-six, while in Massachusetts it was almost the same as in 1890.

Though the average income per capita of the Texans is far less than that of the people in many other States, Texas is growing rich fast. In approximate figures, the value of the property in the State, as assessed for taxation, in 1850 was fifty millions; in 1860 it was three hundred millions; in 1870 one hundred and seventy millions; in 1880 three hundred and eleven millions; in 1890 seven hundred and eighty-two millions; while in 1902 it was one thousand and seventeen millions.

Men are worth more than money. Whatever the wealth or natural resources of a State may be, it is the people who, in the last analysis, are its most essential and interesting element. A few facts concerning the make-up and antecedents of the people of Texas may go a good way towards explaining the Texan character. This is the one Southern State that has really grown by immigration. The white population of Texas at the outbreak of the Revolution was something over twenty thousand. Morfit, the agent sent by Jackson in 1836, estimated the number of Anglo-Americans at thirty thousand. From the time when the figures of the United States census become available, the population at the end of each successive decade is, in round numbers, as follows: in 1850 two hundred and twelve thousand; in 1860 six hundred and four thousand; in 1870 eight hundred and eighteen thousand; in 1880 sixteen hundred thousand; in 1890 nearly two and a quarter millions; in 1900 three million and fifty thousand.

While the larger part of the immigration to Texas has come from the States of the South further east

and northeast, much of it has been from other parts
of the world. It has by no means obeyed the rule
of following parallels. There are few States, in
fact, whose people are so cosmopolitan. Of its
three million and fifty thousand inhabitants in
1900, about fifteen hundred thousand were native
whites, and about five hundred thousand native
negroes. The number of whites not born in the
State was something over nine hundred thousand,
of whom about twenty thousand were from the
North Atlantic States, one hundred and fifty thousand from the South Atlantic, one hundred and
twenty thousand from the North Central, five hundred and thirty thousand from the South Central
other than Texas itself, and six thousand from
the Western. Ten thousand were born under the
United States flag in no specified State or Territory.
The foreign population was one hundred and eighty
thousand, of whom about seventy thousand were
from Mexico, fifty thousand from Germany, nine
thousand from Bohemia, eight thousand from England, seven thousand from Austria, six thousand
from Ireland, four thousand from Italy, four thousand from Sweden, two thousand from France.
The number of Mexicans and Germans born in the
State, and thus classed as natives, is also very large.
This summarized and general analysis will suffice
to show how numerous and how diverse are the
elements of the population of Texas.

Much in the Texan type of character is to be
explained by the process of natural selection which

worked in determining the kind of people carried thither by the earlier movement of the Anglo-Americans towards that section. They were just such as would undertake, of their own will, pioneer work in a country not yet won either from nature or from the Indians, where there was much to dare and much to undergo. There were no gold mines to tempt them, nor any prospect of suddenly acquiring great riches. The motive was simply that of bettering their condition, and of securing a chance, perhaps, to become wealthy as the land they were given should increase in value. The inducements were not such as to attract adventurers, and there were few of these that came. The colonists were mainly poor in worldly goods, but they were brave, hardy, and self-reliant. With the development, however, of the Republic and the State, as the conditions became more settled and the risks grew less and opportunities more abundant, another class was drawn toward Texas. This was composed of shrewd and keen-sighted men of business, watchful for every chance and ready to improve it to the utmost, and especially fit for the development of the commercial interests of any section. It is these especially who have accumulated capital, have built the cities, and have taken the lead in the great industrial enterprises of the State.

Upon the Texas individuality has been left also the stamp of the remarkable experiences that have gone to make up the history of the Republic and the State. Were there not remaining in Texas the descendants of those who died in the Alamo, or of those who followed Houston in the retreat before the Mexicans in 1836, and who finally turned upon them with destructive energy at San Jacinto, the traditions of the revolution could still hardly fail to raise the standard of manhood of the people whose inheritance they have become. The indomitable energy of the colonists in defense of their rights as they understood them, their self-assertion and self-devotion, have undoubtedly left a residuum of influence that is still manifest in the great mass of Texans; nor is it difficult to see in the Texas character surviving traces of the strenuous self-repression and the fierce antipathies of the days of reconstruction that time alone will remove. Yet the people of Texas, boastful as they may be at times, have never been touched by the leaven of the Pharisee.

On the whole, the best outcome of Texas history and the best illustration of the Texas spirit lie in the educational and eleemosynary systems of the State, and the chapter and this book may be fitly closed with a few words concerning them. *Pari passu* with the growth of population and of wealth in the State has grown the feeling of obligation to provide for the care of its defectives and the education of its youth. The first public charitable institution in Texas was that for the blind, which was opened in 1856. It was soon followed by the institute for the deaf and dumb and the asylum for the insane. Within the last few years these institutions have been multiplied and enlarged till now the State may fairly claim to be approximating an adequate and efficient system. The list of establishments now includes four extensive asylums for lunatics, one being especially for epileptics, an institute for the deaf and dumb, one for the blind, one for colored deaf, dumb, and blind, an orphans' home, and a home for Confederate veterans. These, at the limit of their capacity, provide for about thirty-six hundred lunatics, four hundred and fifty white deaf and dumb, one hundred and seventy-five white blind, one hundred colored deaf and dumb or blind, three hundred orphans, and three hundred and twenty Confederate veterans.

The care of defectives, orphans, and veterans, however, would be the prompting of simple humanity, and an extensive system for the purpose might be more the outgrowth of general sympathy than of high social ideals or a clear view of how the government can render most effective service to the people. The best and truest measure, perhaps, of the insight and the social wisdom of any community lies in the perfection of its educational institutions. If Texas is yet too young to claim a place, in this respect, among the very foremost States, there are certainly few that are making such rapid progress. The reader has already seen that education was one of the earliest concerns of the Republic, and that the State showed the same desire and strove to realize it until the outbreak of the Civil War. When reconstruction was over, and the thought and energy of the people of Texas began to return to their accustomed channels, the work of educational development began anew, and was pushed on with great vigor. Since then, much progress has been made towards the establishment of a really good and efficient system of public schools. Most cities and towns of importance have formed independent school districts and levied special taxes for their support. The system of joining state and local effort so as to supplement each other has been so wisely framed and administered as to afford a degree of educational advantage to the poorest communities, and at the same time to foster local responsibility and civic pride.

Along with the common schools, and superposed thereon, has grown up also a system of secondary and higher education. This began with the establishment of the State Agricultural and Mechanical College in 1876. The next step forward was the founding of the Sam Houston Normal Institute in 1879; and the next, the organization of the University of Texas, which was opened to students in 1883. Besides the institutions named the State has another normal school for training white teachers at Denton and still another soon to be opened at San Marcos, one for colored teachers at Prairie View, and a girl's industrial school to begin work shortly at Denton; while in the high schools of the cities and larger towns students expecting to enter the University can obtain preparatory training that is rapidly attaining a high degree of excellence.

The growth of the University has been very gratifying. At the time of its organization in 1883, it opened with a faculty of thirteen officers and instructors of all ranks, and only about two hundred students, who were divided between the academic and the law departments. For the year 1901–1902 the faculties and other officers of the various branches of the University numbered one hundred and ten, and the total enrollment amounted to nearly thirteen hundred.

For all that the State and the independent districts are doing, private educational enterprise continues to flourish in Texas. In the thirteenth biennial report of the superintendent of public instruction (1902) appear statistics of fifty-six private and church schools and colleges, which make quite a creditable showing for private education in the State.

It is, however, rather of educational progress than of the status attained that Texas can boast; and the same is true not only in education, but in most other matters. What has been done is not as significant and hopeful in itself as it is in its promise of more to come. So Texas looks out upon the twentieth century and all future time brimming with courage, energy, and faith.

INDEX

AMERICAN STATESMEN

Biographies of Men famous in the Political History of the United States. Edited by JOHN T. MORSE, JR. Each volume, with portrait, 16mo, gilt top, $1.25. The set, 31 volumes, $38.75; half morocco, $85.25.

Separately they are interesting and entertaining biographies of our most eminent public men; as a series they are especially remarkable as constituting a history of American politics and policies more complete and more useful for instruction and reference than any that I am aware of. — HON. JOHN W. GRIGGS, Ex-United States Attorney-General.

BENJAMIN FRANKLIN. By JOHN T. MORSE, JR.
SAMUEL ADAMS. By JAMES K. HOSMER.
PATRICK HENRY. By MOSES COIT TYLER.
GEORGE WASHINGTON. By HENRY CABOT LODGE. 2 volumes.
JOHN ADAMS. By JOHN T. MORSE, JR.
ALEXANDER HAMILTON. By HENRY CABOT LODGE.
GOUVERNEUR MORRIS. By THEODORE ROOSEVELT.
JOHN JAY. By GEORGE PELLEW.
JOHN MARSHALL. By ALLAN B. MAGRUDER.
THOMAS JEFFERSON. By JOHN T. MORSE, JR.
JAMES MADISON. By SYDNEY HOWARD GAY.
ALBERT GALLATIN. By JOHN AUSTIN STEVENS.
JAMES MONROE. By D. C. GILMAN.
JOHN QUINCY ADAMS. By JOHN T. MORSE, JR.
JOHN RANDOLPH. By HENRY ADAMS.
ANDREW JACKSON. By W. G. SUMNER
MARTIN VAN BUREN. By EDWARD W. SHEPARD.
HENRY CLAY. By CARL SCHURZ. 2 volumes.
DANIEL WEBSTER. By HENRY CABOT LODGE.
JOHN C. CALHOUN. By DR. H. VON HOLST.
THOMAS H. BENTON. By THEODORE ROOSEVELT.
LEWIS CASS. By ANDREW C. MCLAUGHLIN.
ABRAHAM LINCOLN. By JOHN T. MORSE, JR. 2 volumes.
WILLIAM H. SEWARD. By THORNTON K. LOTHROP.
SALMON P CHASE. By ALBERT BUSHNELL HART.
CHARLES FRANCIS ADAMS. By C. F. ADAMS, JR.
CHARLES SUMNER. By MOORFIELD STOREY.
THADDEUS STEVENS. By SAMUEL W. MCCALL.

SECOND SERIES

Biographies of men particularly influential in the recent Political History of the Nation. Each volume, with Portrait, 12mo, $1.25 *net*; postage 12 cents.

This second series is intended to supplement the original list of American Statesmen by the addition of the names of men who have helped to make the history of the United States since the Civil War.

JAMES G. BLAINE. By EDWARD STANWOOD.
JOHN SHERMAN. By THEODORE E. BURTON.
WILLIAM McKINLEY. By T. C. DAWSON.

ULYSSES S. GRANT. By SAMUEL W. MCCALL. In preparation

Other interesting additions to the list to be made in the future.

HOUGHTON MIFFLIN COMPANY

AMERICAN
COMMONWEALTHS

Volumes devoted to such States of the Union as have a striking political, social, or economic history. Each volume, with Map and Index, 16mo, gilt top, $1.25, *net;* postage 12 cents. The set, 19 vols., $23.75; half polished morocco, $52.25.

The books which form this series are scholarly and readable individually; collectively, the series, when completed, will present a history of the nation, setting forth in lucid and vigorous style the varieties of government and of social life to be found in the various commonwealths included in the federal union.

CALIFORNIA. By Josiah Royce.
CONNECTICUT. By Alexander Johnston. (Revised Ed.)
INDIANA. By J. P. Dunn, Jr. (Revised Edition.)
KANSAS. By Leverett W. Spring. (Revised Edition.)
KENTUCKY. By Nathaniel Southgate Shaler.
LOUISIANA. By Albert Phelps.
MARYLAND. By William Hand Browne. (Revised Ed.)
MICHIGAN. By Thomas M. Cooley. (Revised Edition.)
MINNESOTA. By Wm. W. Folwell.
MISSOURI. By Lucien Carr.
NEW HAMPSHIRE. By Frank B. Sanborn.
NEW YORK. By Ellis H. Roberts. 2 vols. (Revised Ed.)
OHIO. By Rufus King. (Revised Edition.)
RHODE ISLAND. By Irving B. Richman.
TEXAS. By George P. Garrison.
VERMONT. By Rowland E. Robinson.
VIRGINIA. By John Esten Cooke. (Revised Edition.)
WISCONSIN. By Reuben Gold Thwaites.

In preparation

GEORGIA. By Ulrich B. Phillips.
ILLINOIS. By John H. Finley.
IOWA. By Albert Shaw.
MASSACHUSETTS. By Edward Channing.
NEW JERSEY. By Austin Scott.
OREGON. By F. H. Hodder.
PENNSYLVANIA. By Talcott Williams.

HOUGHTON MIFFLIN COMPANY